Praise for *Risk*
the first book in the
God's Man Series

"I've always been an adrenaline junkie, so *Risk* instantly appealed to me. This book goes beyond the interesting and engaging descriptive stories to provide much needed prescriptive insight to enable men to live more boldly and powerfully. If you're up for being challenged in significant ways, read this book."

—MARK SANBORN, president of Sanborn and Associates Inc.
and author of *The Fred Factor: How Passion in Your Work
and Life Can Turn the Ordinary into the Extraordinary*

"Understanding the significance of the Christian message is of such great importance there cannot be too many ways to bring it to our attention. *Risk* is certain to inspire readers who long to give their all to a mighty cause, but who might miss the message if it were presented in a less passionate way."

—KEN BLANCHARD, co-author of *The One-Minute Manager*
and *The Secret*

"Shocking are the Scripture's stories of men that took a risk! So are the modern-day accounts of men changing the world for God by taking risks. And then there's you… Are you risking it? This is a man's book for men—men of God ready to rip into the ends of the age. Dive into *Risk*!"

—DR. WAYNE CORDEIRO, senior pastor of New Hope
Christian Fellowship Oahu and author of *Doing Church
As a Team* and *Culture Shift*

"*Risk* is a book for men. It challenges us to faith, courage, and commitment. Kenny Luck tells the inspiring stories of men who risked everything to follow God. Don't miss this exciting and riveting challenge. It will stir your soul to action."

—DR. JERRY FALWELL, Liberty University in Lynchburg, Virginia

"*Risk* is a must-read for any man seeking significant change in his life. The book has great depth and momentum. Kenny Luck clearly communicates the message of what it means to completely sell out to God. Thank you, Kenny. I pray that all men everywhere will take the risk and trust God for everything."

—DAVEY BUHL, director of men's ministry at Christ Church at Grove Farm

DREAM WORKBOOK
PUBLISHED BY WATERBROOK PRESS
12265 Oracle Boulevard, Suite 200
Colorado Springs, Colorado 80921
A division of Random House Inc.

ISBN 978-1-57856-992-2

Printed in the United States of America
2007—First Edition

10 9 8 7 6 5 4 3 2 1

SPECIAL SALES
Most WaterBrook books are available in special quantity discounts when purchased in bulk by corporations, organizations, and special interest groups. Custom imprinting or excerpting can also be done to fit special needs. For information, please e-mail SpecialMarkets@WaterBrookPress.com or call 1-800-603-7051.

dream

workbook

Have You Caught
God's Vision?

kenny luck

WATERBROOK
PRESS

contents

how to use this workbook

This workbook, a companion to *Dream,* is designed to be used in three ways:

1. *Personal workbook.* If you want to understand God's dreams for you and grow in faith, you will enjoy unpacking challenging material and applying it to your own journey as God's man. Each week's session in the workbook contains two sections for personal study and action: Dream Analysis and Dream Discipline (includes Scripture to memorize during the week's study). If you read the assigned chapters in *Dream,* which I recommend, plan on investing at least two hours in each lesson.

2. *One-on-one study.* This approach is for you and an accountability partner. This may be the best way to get the most benefit from this workbook. Each week, you and your partner will individually study the material. Then you will get together to discuss the content and work as a team on some one-on-one questions and exercises (Dream Debriefing—Man to Man).

3. *Small group discussion guide.* Men appreciate getting together to hear each other's opinions, share some laughs, study the Word, encourage one another, and pray. Each session of the *Dream Workbook* includes a list of questions (Dream Interpretation—Small Group Discussion) that are intended for a gathering of men. These discussions will be most rewarding if every participant completes the personal workbook study before the small group meeting.

The end of each session includes the suggested readings and assignment for the next week.

No matter how you use the *Dream Workbook,* you will have many opportunities to go deeper in your faith and realize the rewards of understanding God's dreams for you. However, you will experience maximum results if you participate in every element: personal workbook, one-on-one study, and small group discussion.

The workbook includes ample space for you to write your answers, comments, and questions. A special page—the Dream Journal—follows the conclusion of each session. This is a place for you to write any ideas, conclusions, challenges, and personal insights that you found meaningful in that week's session.

The *Dream Workbook* is designed for an eight-week time frame. However, if it takes you longer to complete the study, don't worry. Take all the time you need. It is not unusual for a group to spend two or three meetings completing one lesson. Go for depth over distance—every time.

Before you begin each study, commit your time to God. Ask the Holy Spirit to illumine your mind, guide your heart, and energize your spirit as you read each section and answer each question.

Above all, please adapt this workbook so that it truly works for you. This is your workbook, your invitation to know God better, your opportunity to explore God's dreams for you.

introduction

Greatness has always been a fantasy of mine. I suppose I started dreaming about greatness the same day I discovered Batman. He was larger than life and doing larger than average superhero work. Once I got the plastic Batman helmet, it was all over. Complete identity shift.

As I grew (and discovered football), my dreams changed. I became even more acquainted with the whole concept of glory and found ways to jump off, over, and through chasms or obstacles. Why? To possess and be around glory feels good.

I have discovered, though, that there is a cloud that darkens the blue sky of boyhood dreaming: reality. When reality hits, the dreams that soar through the stratosphere of our imagination too often stall, crash, and burn. Then, as we make our way through adolescence and graduate to manhood, new dreams are born. Our big boy dreams tend toward beautiful women, fast cars, big bucks jobs, exotic vacations, TV screens the size of plywood sheets, skybox season tickets, or a retirement condo on the coast. And if we can't achieve those, there's always fantasy.

I'm here to tell you that God has something bigger in mind. Our Father's dreams for His boys involve advancing the only kingdom built to last. God has warrior dreams for His men; we have battles of cosmic and eternal importance to fight and win.

Have you ever stopped to consider what God's dreams are for you? In this companion workbook to my book *Dream,* I have created a study that I hope will refresh and reenergize your enthusiasm for pursuing the plans God has for you (see Jeremiah 29:11).

I desperately want to pursue what God has in mind for me. If you have the same desire, let's make our way together into a deeper understanding of God's dreams for us.

Dreaming big with you,
KENNY LUCK
kennyl@everymanministries.com

born to dream

This week's session is based on chapter 1, "When God Gives Glasses," in Dream.

Men are dreamers.

Oh, I know, life throws wicked curves, and it may seem that all our dreams have perished. But is that really true? I don't think so. I believe that our dreams are like the magma of a volcano.

📖 Look at yourself and the men around you and think, *Kilahuea.* Kilahuea (kill-uh-WAY-uh) is the most active lava-producing volcano in the world. It used to be dormant. In Hawaii, it started exploding in 1953 and again in 1983. It hasn't stopped flowing lava since, according to the U.S. Geological Survey. All men are Kilahuea, bursting with bright orange visions and dreams that will challenge reality and shake up the landscape forever. Some men have magma close to the surface. Some have theirs buried deep. But make no mistake—it's there, it's alive, and it's put there by God. 📖

What about you? Is the magma of your dreams flowing or trapped deep inside? My prayer is that as you, and several of your friends, grapple with the content of this workbook, God's dream for your life will erupt for His glory and the advancement of the cause of Christ. Our world desperately needs men living out the dreams God has burned into their hearts.

Before we get started, I want you to be aware that throughout this workbook you will encounter excerpts from my book *Dream*. These will be identified by this icon: . These sections were selected to stimulate your thinking and assist you in gaining more benefit from the workbook. You will obtain the most insight, however, if you read the companion chapters in their entirety. I will not be able to repeat many of the illustrations that appear in the book. These stories put meat on the bones when it comes to grasping a full understanding of what it means to be God's men pursuing God's dreams for us.

✦ Dream Analysis

When I was a boy, I had no shortage of dreams. Many of my fantasies included heroics in sports. I dreamed I was the tailback who, after breaking five tackles, shifts into another gear and pulls away from the gasping defensive backs on my way to the end zone. Dreaming like that seemed as natural as breathing.

1. What were some of the dreams you had as a boy?

2. Which, if any, of these dreams have come true?

📖 You were made to dream creative visions, because you were hardwired for more.

You don't have to accept less or feel bad about wanting to transcend reality. You're Daddy's boy—you are made to be great like Him....

God's vision for [you] is different from [your] vision....

When life isn't going well, we long for a better life. Heck, even when life seems to be perfect, we long for more. Admit it! We feel this pull to rearrange reality, to experience freedom, to gratify deep longings inside. 📖

3. What have you sensed in yourself that reveals you were hardwired for more—more in life than only day-to-day, normal living?

4. How would you describe the "more" that you long for in your life? Take your time to answer—and be specific.

📖 God's vision for you is solid, invincible, and has been in place for a long time. It is an oak tree. It is unstoppable. Only arrogance or ignorance would attempt to displace it, try to cheat it or ignore it. And yet we do. We presume to design what we will become in Him. We chase our fantasies over His chosen vision. We forecast and fashion our lives in our own image. We reengineer ourselves for cultural acceptability. We shape our dreams around our own insecurities and dysfunctional tendencies.

And then there is the fatal error: we take God's plan for our lives and make it something to be conquered. 📖

5. What do you believe is God's vision for your life?

6. In what ways, if any, have you chased your own vision for your life instead of aligning yourself with God's vision for your life?

Encounter with Reality

📖 I don't know exactly when it happened, but time was not a friend to my early visions of greatness. I had to grow up. We all did. As this happened, our visions of glory were tempered and morphed to reflect the realities of life. Time wasn't always on our side. The events of life got in the way—divorce, death, disappointment, unreasonable standards. We started to lose hope. Our loneliness split our loyalty and disintegrated our faith in real relationships.

The pure, ideal visions simply went away and were replaced with insecurities and fears which led not to dreams but to fantasies that soothed our hurts. Escape and relief relegated greatness to just getting by. Glory was simply not reality anymore.

Reality won. Glory was lost. 📖

1. Has time been a friend to your early visions of greatness or glory? Why or why not?

2. What events in your growing-up years were the most influential in aborting or postponing your dreams?

3. Sadly, many of us find inappropriate ways to soothe our hurts. If this is what happened to you, what fantasies or other substitutes have you used to relieve your pain?

📖 This war between reality and glory happens in cycles throughout our lives. The magma of our dreams pushes its way up again. There are a few sparks. Going off to college. Graduation. Career. Promotions. All visions of heading off for glory. Then reality nudges in, reshapes things and blocks our path to real glory. Our vision gets tackled for a loss. It's fourth and long, and we have to surrender the ball. The energy drains out. Gravity wins. Earth pulls us down. We may have heard the rumblings, but we never saw the bright orange magma, the awesome power we had planned to see. 📖

4. In your life so far, what would you list as glory moments—those times when you felt the sweet smell of success?

5. Why do you think reality nudges in and blocks the path to real glory?

📖 Reality says that 5 percent of life is extremely satisfying. Another 5 percent is extremely disappointing. The rest—the other 90 percent is just life, plain peanut butter and jelly. The dream for me and the glory that goes with it reside somewhere else, in some other life, some other place, far away from the peanut-butter-and-jelly life. It's somewhere out there for the select few and uberspiritual.

In Africa maybe.

Then a little voice whispers, *Or is it?* 📖

I keep asking that the God of our Lord Jesus Christ, the glorious Father, may give you the Spirit of wisdom and revelation, so that you may know him better. I pray also that the eyes of your heart may be enlightened in order that you may know the hope to which he has called you, the riches of his glorious inheritance in the saints, and his incomparably great power for us who believe. (Ephesians 1:17–19)

6. Why do you believe—or not believe—that God has great plans for you and has destined you for glory?

7. What might be involved in the process of enlightening the eyes of your heart?

Grasping God's Dreams

📖 It's time for a fresh vision of who He has called you to be. It's time to seek the glory which is yours for the taking right where you are. Embrace these five DREAM principles for every God's man:

- **D**ecide to let God decide for you.
- **R**eside in the glory of your reality.
- **E**xchange your vision for God's.
- **A**ccept God's process.
- **M**ove your borders in continual growth. 📖

Desire God's Dream for You

📖 The minute I start letting feelings, culture, or others decide what defines my dream, I am cooked as God's man. Jesus is our Master Baker on this one. "My Father, if it is possible, may this *cup* be taken from me. Yet not as I will, but as you will" (Matthew 26:39). Jesus let His Father decide what the dream for His life on earth would be. The dream didn't depend on His circumstances, His rights, His parents, His friends, His critics, or His feelings. It's no surprise then that the exact dream God has for you is in the mold of His Son. "For those God foreknew he also predestined to be conformed to the likeness of his Son, that he might be the firstborn among many brothers" (Romans 8:29). For every God's man ever born, this has been the plan, and this is the process we are all engaged in: becoming like our firstborn Brother, Jesus. 📖

1. To what extent have other factors, such as feelings, parents, culture, or friends, distracted you from seeking to fulfill God's dream for your life?

2. If you are to pursue God's dream for you, what areas of your character and behavior will need to mature the most?

Reality Is Where Glory Resides

📖 Your reality is God's glory. Everything that is happening in your life—especially the stuff you want to keep a secret—is an ingredient in God's greatness. You might be thinking, *I don't want God to use that!* God's reply is, *That is exactly what I want to use.* God is eager to use your now-life, not your cleaned-up version. To fuel the dream, He prefers struggles over strengths. One gives Him glory, the other gives you glory....

"As he went along, he saw a man blind from birth. His disciples asked him, 'Rabbi, who sinned, this man or his parents, that he was born blind?' 'Neither this man nor his parents sinned,' said Jesus, 'but this happened so that the work of God might be displayed in his life'" (John 9:1–3).

Reality is where glory resides. 📖

3. Describe a situation, a character flaw, a foolish mistake, or similar issue in your life when God used your stinky stuff for His glory.

Exchange the Vision

Some men envisioned their lives would turn out a certain way, but those plans fell apart. Some of these guys feel ripped-off and angry because they were supposed to achieve their dads' visions. They felt controlled and forfeited their chances to choose. A lot of men were wounded so badly by their dads, they chased the opposite vision in response. Resenting or trying to please those wounding fathers only led to anger, and they ended up becoming just like them. Others were trained by tradition. Mom and Dad taught them that their lives should look and feel a certain way, and that's exactly what they turned out to be. Tradition triumphs over the individual. But that's not the man's life, it's his parents'. Still other men have built their lives to directly reflect their insecurities and masculine fears. These guys attach to cultural definitions of success, stockpiling pleasure, power, or possessions to gain what they could not find in their early relationships. This kind of life almost always fragments relationships and leaves men starving for intimacy and connection. In each of these cases, the dream leads to emotional, relational, and spiritual bondage. They are the false dreams that involve chasing, wishing, and hoping. They are not Christlikeness. They are empty and void of spiritual power because they are the man-made fantasies, not the God-made dream.

4. What category from the previous would you put yourself in? Have you been able to pursue God's dream without much opposition or distraction?

5. Which of the cultural definitions of success—money, career, pleasure, toys, power—has tempted you the most to not pursue God's dream for you?

Accept God's Process

📖 God is not very product oriented. That's a bummer for most men, including me. We like to look at what we've done....

Surrendering to the process is not a masculine gift. In fact, the Bible is littered with stories of leaders who ran ahead of God because they were impatient. And they paid the price. Both ancient and modern men of faith can relate to the proverb, "There is a way that seems right to a man, but in the end it leads to death" (Proverbs 14:12). When the timing and means are not as we would have it, or the results feel unjust or unacceptable, we tend to fight the process. Fighting an unjust process is not a bad thing. Fighting God's process of making you the man He created you to be is disastrous. Avoiding that sinkhole takes guts and a belief that God is more capable of deciding what's needed and best for you at any given moment.

God's dream of molding you into the image of Christ will involve discomfort, conflict, loss, and pain. Stick with me. 📖

6. What experiences have you had during the process of being molded into the image of Christ that have been difficult for you?

Move the Borders of Your Growth Continuously

God's man prays the brave prayers of continual growth. Prayers like Job's emerge when he opens his life up to God's inspection and gives his Maker freedom to rewire his life. He keeps moving the borders, giving God more and more freedom to change him.

"If I have walked in falsehood or my foot has hurried after deceit—let God weigh me in honest scales and he will know that I am blameless—if my steps have turned from the path, if my heart has been led by my eyes, or if my hands have been defiled, then may others eat what I have sown, and may my crops be uprooted.... Then may my wife grind another man's grain, and may other men sleep with her" (Job 31:5–8, 10).

Whoa, mama! That is what you call the open-kimono prayer. The dude is naked before God because he wants growth and spiritual integrity. It's a bring-it-on confession and prayer.

7. In what areas of your life do you think God desires to move the borders so you can more freely and fully seek His dream for you?

What will be the results if you keep moving your borders of growth?

- new insights
- less selfish impulse
- new character
- less confusion
- new conduct
- less confession
- new spirit

- less collateral damage
- new growth
- less disappointment
- more impact
- less regret
- more motivation
- less frustration

No extra charge for the deep, gasping adrenaline rushes and unforgettable testimonies of God's power, which will also be yours. Read that list again. Go ahead. God says, *That's what I want for you.*

God's dream for us is not something we chase; it's something we become....

God's dream for your life is not external, designed to impress. It's not internal, a value or a purpose. It's not even a spiritual discipline or set of beliefs. God's dream for you is a heaven-owned vision of greatness, a God's man image built upon that of the God-Man.

You have known this and felt it inside of you ever since you were a little boy. It's time for all of us to recapture it.

Dream Discipline

Each session, as you complete the Dream Analysis section of the *Dream Workbook,* I will ask you to spend a few minutes summarizing what we have covered. An important part of living a sold-out life for Christ is to grasp the meaning of the Word of God and capitalize on its power—just like Jesus did throughout His life on earth. I urge you to memorize a crucial verse in each session, which will always be highlighted under the Remember heading.

Remember

> And we, who with unveiled faces all reflect the Lord's glory, are being transformed into his likeness with *ever-increasing glory*, which comes from the Lord, who is the Spirit. (2 Corinthians 3:18)

Reflect

1. What do you think it means to reflect the Lord's glory with unveiled faces?

2. As you begin this workbook on God's dreams for you, how would you like to be increasingly transformed into the likeness of Christ?

Respond

This week, as you go about your daily life, consider how your activities, thoughts, and attitudes are either advancing or hindering the completion of God's dreams for you. Make notes here.

 Dream Debriefing (Man to Man)

Becoming a fully effective God's man requires you to have an honest, strong accountability relationship with at least one godly man. In each session I will list several questions for you to ask each other—ideally at a time when you get together each week to find out how life is going, feast on the Word, and pray.

Take turns asking each other these questions:

1. When you were a boy, what were your dreams about what you wanted to do when you grew up?

2. Looking back now from an adult perspective, which of those boyhood dreams do you think were a prompting from God to respond to His call on your life?

3. Share personal needs and requests, and pray for each other.

 Dream Interpretation (Small Group Discussion)

1. Dreaming seems to come easily to boys. Ask each member of the group to share some of the dreams he had during childhood.

2. How do we determine what God's dreams are for our lives?

3. Are God's dreams for us necessarily different than our own dreams? Why or why not?

4. Take turns describing what each man thinks is the magma in his life. Is the magma flowing or bottled up inside?

5. In *Dream* we read, "God's dream for us is not something we chase; it's something we become." In the group, discuss how this has been true in your lives.

6. As God's men and brothers in Christ, how can we encourage each other to stay on course in realizing God's dream for each of us?

☀ Dream and Do

Here's what needs to happen before the next small group meeting:

1. Complete your personal study of session 2, which includes reading chapters 2, 3, and 4 in *Dream*.

2. Meet with your accountability partner.

3. Accomplish the reflection requested under Respond in the Dream Discipline section on page 38.

4. Record any of your observations in the Dream Journal.

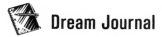 **Dream Journal**

_____

_____

_____

_____

_____

_____

_____

_____

leaking like Jesus

This week's session is based on chapter 2, "Leaking Jesus," chapter 3, "No Neon," and chapter 4, "Not So With You," in Dream.

Leaking is the theme of this session.

The leaking we will discuss is the inevitable flow of character qualities that flow out of each of us.

In *Dream* I share the story of how my daughter's diaper once sprung a memorable leak that flooded my trousers. It was a stinky leak. Some of us leak stinky character on the people around us.

When we have Jesus filling us up with His life, our leaks smell good and make life better for others. That's what we're after—spreading an aroma that is sweet, enriches the lives of others, and brings glory to God.

✧ Dream Analysis

📖 In life, what's inside will eventually come out. And there's nothing you can do to stop it. We do our best to prevent spills and leaks. Diapers, Tupperware, and window caulking all prevent undesirable seepage of stuff into the protected spaces of our lives. But when it comes to our character—the stuff inside that guides critical decision making—there are no controls to stop the leaks. And frequently, we leak onto others.

It goes like this: Signals and stimuli inevitably trigger a flood of your character, which spills into your everyday interactions. These spills have a shaping influence on those around us. Jesus put it this way: "The good man brings good things out of the good stored up in him, and the evil man brings evil things out of the evil stored up in him" (Matthew 12:35).

The big question is, what sort of character are you leaking? 📖

1. List some situations—good and bad—where your character leaked out onto those around you.

2. What causes us to leak good character qualities sometimes and bad character qualities other times?

📖 We can't stop the leaking, but God's dream changes what's coming out. In short, He prefers the water main of His character to transform our stink into a new, pleasing expression. He wants to replace the leaking sin and selfishness with the redeeming character of Christ. 📖

3. Make a list of the places (work, family, health club, and so on) where you have an opportunity to let your water main of character get others wet.

4. Review the list you wrote for the last question and circle the situations where, with the assistance of the Holy Spirit, you need to improve the quality of your character leaking.

📖 The titanic irony is that our human weaknesses provide occasions for the triumph of divine power. It did that night in my family, and it will in your life when you understand exactly what God's dream is: that you leak Jesus more and leak self less. One expression of character makes healthy relationships. The other produces harm. One makes you better. The other makes messes. One involves surrender. The other involves slavery. One brings love, sacrifice, and salvation to a dying world. The other brings disconnection and destruction. 📖

5. How have you seen God's power demonstrated in an area of personal weakness?

The Ultimate Character Quality

If we are to live God's dream, we need to welcome the process of letting go of the ideas, behaviors, and attitudes that take our focus off the right and righteous path.

> Therefore, since we are surrounded by such a huge crowd of witnesses to the life of faith, let us strip off every weight that slows us down, especially the sin that so easily trips us up. And let us run with endurance the race God has set before us. (Hebrews 12:1, NLT)

That is why God's man…needs to have a confident grip of God in his life. When we are disconnected from a clear understanding of God's abilities, God's love, God's attitude toward us, and God's dream for us, we simply cannot let go of these hindrances:

- the need to be noticed
- the need to prove our worth
- images
- the need to be first
- trying to please people
- self
- prejudice
- hurts

1. Using this list as a guide, what areas in your life are difficult to release? Why?

2. How can you go about connecting strongly to God's abilities, love, and attitude toward you?

God's dream for us includes making us authentically humble. We know this because the quality of humility was strong in our hero—Jesus. Jesus didn't need to showboat in the end zone. Jesus didn't need five minutes of fame. Jesus knew He was the Son of the Father and that's all that mattered. Jesus did not need neon. And God's plan for all of His other sons is the same.

> [This is] the dream every God's man feels deeply in the magma of his soul: to act nobly and humbly before God and man....
>
> For God's man, greatness on earth starts with humble surrender—giving yourself to Christ and refusing to resist His power. Everybody starts there. "Humble yourselves, therefore, under God's mighty hand, that he may lift you up in due time" (1 Peter 5:6).

3. In our culture, how would most people define *humility*?

4. What's your definition of humility?

📖 The axis of humility is internal.... This is because, at its roots, true Christ-based humility in a man combines a modest opinion of one's own importance with an excessively high estimation of the importance of God and people. 📖

5. Would you say that the character of most men tends toward pride or humility? Give reasons for your answer.

6. Generally, how do you regard yourself in comparison to others?

The first step to developing Christlike humility is humbly unburdening yourself to Christ. You cannot possess Christ unless you are willing to risk humble surrender to Him. Jesus liked the show-how method of developing humility. Take a look back at his words from Matthew [11:28–30]:

- I do; you watch.
- I do; you participate.
- We do it together.
- You do; I watch.

This is the invitation to the "humblee" (you) to have a relationship with your "Humbler." God and man, Savior and sinner, Brother-King and servant join to learn to become like Him.

7. What is required to humbly surrender to Christ?

8. What does Christ promise when you humbly surrender to Him?

9. Why do you think Jesus's yoke is easy and His burden is light?

Humility costs us something. We are not naturally humble; we are naturally proud. Humility requires that we crucify self-centeredness, arrogance, and pride. That's not easy.

    📖 We have to get on our face to see His face. We have to get low in our estimation of ourselves to get high in God's estimation of us. We have to reflect humility to reveal Christ on earth. When we take this step, we are able to do more for God and people than we ever dreamed—just like the King. 📖

10. Do you feel you are humble before God? Take a few minutes and pray about this topic. Record your thoughts here.

The Humility of Jesus

To live an authentically humble life, we need to lock in like radar on the example Jesus gave us. He showed us how to do this:

> Think of yourselves the way Christ Jesus thought of himself. He had equal status with God but didn't think so much of himself that he had to cling to the advantages of that status no matter what. Not at all. When the time came, he set aside the privileges of deity and took on the status of a slave, became human! Having become human, he stayed human. It was an incredibly humbling process. He didn't claim special privileges. Instead, he lived a selfless, obedient life and then died a selfless, obedient death—and the worst kind of death at that—a crucifixion. Because of that obedience, God lifted him high and honored him far beyond anyone or anything, ever, so that all created beings in heaven and on earth—even those long ago dead and buried—will bow in worship before this Jesus Christ, and call out in praise that he is the Master of all, to the glorious honor of God the Father. (Philippians 2:5–11, MSG)

1. What impresses you the most about Jesus's humility?

2. Worship is a common response when we think about what Christ did by humbling Himself. Write some of your own thoughts of thanksgiving and worship as you reflect on the incredible service and sacrifice of the Lord Jesus.

It's Not All About Us

Ultimately, God's dream for us is not all about us. We have an important role in a larger dream, a bigger story—God's plan of the ages. This means that our humility, just as it was with Jesus, is intended to make us better at serving others. This is what genuine humility does in relationships:

It is an emotional posture that makes the people in your presence feel unburdened, light, and connected to you all at the same time. Your presentation is unforced but strong.… In a personal encounter, the possessor of humility disappears as an emotional obstacle to the other person and leaves two powerful forces in their place: God's presence and the other person's importance. Think Jesus and prostitute. Feel the interaction between Jesus and the woman at the well. Revisit Jesus and the lepers. Reread about Jesus and the man born blind. What did they all experience? They all stood in God's presence and felt safe and connected to God. Humbling, isn't it?

To the lonely, marginalized, burdened, stressed, or frenzied, a humble God's man is who they need. That is why Jesus so liberally offered His humility to us—it is refreshing!

1. Think of the genuinely humble people you know or have known. What thoughts and feelings do you have when you are with these people?

📖 Will you be the dad who uses his position to intimidate, demand, and threaten? Or will you be the man in the family who leads out of service more than position? Will you be the man who possesses wealth for his own pleasure? Or will you be the man who gives God control of your finances for His pleasure? Will you be the man who says, *I deserve better than this*? Or will you be God's man who says, *I'm willing to wait for Your timing on this one, Lord*? The languages of entitlement, conditions, and selfishness are not spoken in the land of humility. 📖

2. This is a good time to prayerfully ask God to help you develop true humility in the relationships where the humility of Christ is a challenge.

Faithful Servant

Humility and service to others are like blood brothers. Jesus was the consummate humble servant. That's our destiny as well.

📖 "For we are God's workmanship, created in Christ Jesus to do good works, which God prepared in advance for us to do" (Ephesians 2:10). It's weird to think about my story being God's artistic expression, but that's exactly what it is for God's man. Our lives are God's workmanship and the choices we make are a part of the play he is writing. What's inconceivable to me is that I get to take part in the final scene by the choices I make now. 📖

1. What are the ramifications of knowing that you are God's workmanship?

2. What do you believe are the good works God has prepared for you to do?

📖 It's like man to want to be served. It's like the Son of Man to serve. It's like God's man to reflect the Son of Man.

"Jesus called them together and said, 'You know that the rulers of the Gentiles lord it over them, and their high officials exercise authority over them. Not so with you. Instead, whoever wants to become great among you must be your servant, and whoever wants to be first must be your slave—just as the Son of Man did not come to be served, but to serve, and to give his life as a ransom for many'" (Matthew 20:25–28).

We could get lost in a lot of great theology on this, but for our purposes, there are six words we must focus on in this verse to get to this aspect of Christ-likeness. They are "just as the Son of Man."…

The disciples felt the same thing for Jesus. They aspired to be like Him. They saw Him in action. They made Him the object. But frequently, they skipped the last part—imitation. They replaced that with selfish ambition. They confused their greatness with what made Jesus great. They got into arguments and disagreements over who would be appointed to a cabinet position in the Jesus administration. Even though they watched Him heal the sick, serve the outcasts, and preach the kingdom, they weren't getting it. They attached themselves to the activity His service produced and not to Him.…

If they wanted to be great, they needed get one thing straight: you are never greater than when you are acting in the favor of others.…

In Jesus we see…the Authority served, and He preferred to do it in person. Watch Him in the Gospels. Study Him. He shows up, He counsels, He touches, He heals, He casts out demons, He mentors men, He encourages, He makes breakfast, He hugs the kids. Jesus breaks the rules to serve in person.…

You follow the King who serves. His dream for you is to join Him.

Leaking Like Jesus

By now, I trust you are resolved as God's man to allow the character of Jesus Christ to leak out of you and into your spheres of influence. This is God's dream for you—to bear His likeness.…

No matter where you are in your spiritual journey, study the life of Jesus to imitate how He interacts with people. In the end, your goal is new character expressed in new conduct that impacts people and brings new life.... The full dream is that we would be willing to sacrifice it all—to be crucified with Christ in order to point others to Him. 📖

1. What qualities of Jesus would you like to see more of in yourself?

2. Ask the Lord to point out some areas in your life where you need to sacrifice something about you in order to gain Christ and that impact for God.

The rest of our journey in this workbook is going to center on the character of Christ so that we can accommodate more of it in our own lives through faith and in partnership with the Holy Spirit. I pray that as you move forward, you would do it in a spirit of partnership with the Holy Spirit. How do you do that? Simply ask for

Him to reveal, convict, and lead you through His promptings, revelations and, more important, your circumstances that clearly call you *out* and Christ *in*.

 ## Dream Discipline

Remember

> For we are to God the aroma of Christ among those who are being saved and those who are perishing. To the one we are the smell of death; to the other, the fragrance of life. (2 Corinthians 2:15–16)

Reflect

1. Describe what you think the aroma of Christ is.

2. When did you realize that Jesus had become a fragrance of life instead of a fragrance of death?

Respond

Think of one person you interact with on a daily basis who does not know Jesus. Pray now that during the time you go through this workbook, you will have the opportunity to be the aroma of Christ to that person. Explain your thoughts here.

Dream Debriefing (Man to Man)

Take turns asking each other these questions:

1. What did you think of the idea of leaking character discussed in this session? For the most part, what qualities of character—good and bad—leak out of you?
2. What areas of your life do you need to strengthen so that others see more of Christ and less of you?
3. Share personal needs and requests. Pray for each other.

Dream Interpretation (Small Group Discussion)

1. Rick Warren once said, "People often use the phrase 'like father, like son' to refer to family resemblance. When people see my likeness in my kids it pleases me. God wants his children to bear his image and likeness, too." What qualities of His image and likeness do you think God wants to see in us—His sons?

2. In *Dream* we read, "Your goal is new character expressed in new conduct that impacts people and brings new life." How did Jesus bring life to others? Think of as many examples as possible.

3. Scripture says that we have been "crucified with Christ" (Galatians 2:20). In our lives today, what does being crucified with Christ mean?

4. The bottom line is that God wants each of us to be like Jesus. Ask each person in the group to share one area in his life where he wants to become more like Christ. Close in a "prayer of agreement," presenting all of these requests to God and asking that He accomplish these positive changes in everyone.

Dream and Do

Here's what needs to happen before the next small group meeting:

1. Complete your personal study of session 3, which includes reading chapters 5 and 6 in *Dream*.

2. Meet with your accountability partner.

3. Accomplish the task you listed under Respond in the Dream Discipline section on page 53.

4. Record any of your observations in the Dream Journal.

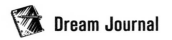 **Dream Journal**

_____

_____

_____

_____

_____

_____

_____

_____

_____

_____

_____

_____

delayed joy

This week's session is based on chapter 5, "Taking the Hit," and chapter 6, "Fully Qualified," in Dream.

Delayed gratification isn't a popular behavior these days. In this session, I would like to consider an important type of delayed gratification: suffering. Followers of Christ must develop the qualities of sacrifice and suffering to yield a reward—later. In fact, much later.

As with all aspects of right living, Jesus provided the example for this. He lived with His heart and head on earth, but I believe He had His spiritual eyes trained on heaven. The Bible says that Jesus was willing to die a shameful death on the cross because of the joy He knew awaited Him (see Hebrews 12:2). That's the best kind of delayed gratification—living a righteous life on earth that prepares you for the rewards and satisfaction of heaven.

I call this delayed joy.

✦ Dream Analysis

Why is it so hard to wait? Do men have trouble developing the virtue of patience?

📖 Men hate to defer pleasure. Wait for something? Oh, man, sign me up! (Cough, hack.)

We are creatures of the moment because we are creatures of the flesh. And the flesh knows only one space-time continuum—*here, now.* Yet if I have a certainty of a future payout, a promise that the cavalry is coming, a definite delivery date of the dream, I can endure a great deal. 📖

1. Do you agree that men hate to defer pleasure? Explain your answer.

2. How patient are you in waiting for a dream to become reality?

📖 For God's dream to be realized in your life, the training is more about endurance than quickness. We are called to endure a great deal and sacrifice experiences, moments, and seasons for a payout that may not come in this life. Why? Because endurance through sacrifice was Jesus's character and expression. 📖

3. What sacrifices have you made in order to realize God's dream for you?

📖 To want Christ means to want to become a man who can sacrifice whatever and whenever. And when we make our peace with that, God's dream for us makes progress. Any attempt to blend the dreams of earth with the dream of God in Christ will force you into losing yardage for the kingdom, and you'll be struggling to kick field goals instead of scoring touchdowns. Trying to do both doesn't lead to the Super Bowl of significance. 📖

4. When have you tried "to blend the dreams of earth with the dream of God" in your life? What were the results?

📖 The good news is that God does not ask us to sacrifice for sacrifice's sake (masochism). He "incentivizes" us. Jesus laid out the incentive structure: "But seek first his kingdom and his righteousness, and all these things will be given to you as well" (Matthew 6:33). To do that involves acts of self-limitation on a continuous basis.…

And when we self-limit for the sake of God's plans, the strong and simple promise (according to Jesus) is that our sacrifices will be honored by God in

His time, His way. That's how Jesus lived His life and how He wants us to live ours.

The "not as I will, but as you will" life is a life of self-limitation for a cause and for a payoff. 📖

5. In your daily life, what does it mean for you to seek first His kingdom and His righteousness?

6. How have you seen God come through on His promise to bless you when you seek His kingdom and righteousness first?

📖 A defining characteristic for every God's man seeking greatness is this: he sacrifices to secure a blessing. Not to sacrifice is to forfeit the reward. He is either in a condition of gaining or losing rewards based on what he is giving up. The strong encouragement, example, and experience of Christ is deeply connected to our own willingness to live a life of continuous sacrifice—a life driven by the solid expectation that our sacrifices for Him on earth will be richly rewarded.

Sacrifice and glory held a symbiotic power for the Son of God. They were two separate and unique experiences that were mysteriously working together for present greatness. This same connection between present sacrifice and future glory is meant to be equally in you as you seek greatness in God's power. 📖

7. Are you aware of any sacrifices God wants you to make now?

Therefore, since we are surrounded by such a huge crowd of witnesses to the life of faith, let us strip off every weight that slows us down, especially the sin that so easily trips us up. And let us run with endurance the race God has set before us. We do this by keeping our eyes on Jesus, the champion who initiates and perfects our faith. *Because of the joy awaiting him, he endured the cross, disregarding its shame.* Now he is seated in the place of honor beside God's throne. Think of all the hostility he endured from sinful people; then you won't become weary and give up. (Hebrews 12:1–3, NLT)

📖 Every one of these you give up for your relationship with God is an opportunity to bring Him glory:

- an attitude
- a behavior
- a response
- a comfort
- a right to strike back
- a feeling
- an impulse
- a chance to control

- a grab for power
- a portion of your time
- a pattern of your old life
- a financial bonus
- a freedom
- a way of doing something
- a golden opportunity 📖

8. Review the list you just read. Circle any items that you feel led to give up. Talk to the Father about your decisions. Thank Him now for the blessings that will come—on earth or in heaven.

Jesus was rich with sacrifice. He sacrificed His time, energy, and efforts. He sacrificed the comforts of home to connect with people. He sacrificed recognition of men for reconciliation of men to God. He sacrificed energy to take care of others, trusting that God would replenish Him at the proper time. He sacrificed His right to get even with His killers. He sacrificed earthly recognition, comfort, approval, pleasures, power, and possessions. He did so knowing that His sacrifices were not unnoticed. More, He knew that beyond recognition would be celebration. He knew He was scoring touchdowns for God on earth versus sitting out, losing yardage, or settling for field goals. He was even hungry enough to go all the way and lay down the costliest sacrifice of all upon the altar of others' free will, and didn't try to force anyone into heaven.

Every sacrifice for God is a touchdown. Big or small. His dream for you is to make a man who is willing to do what is required for the kingdom—in a marriage, at work, in a trauma, in the third world.

9. In your experience, what is one way you have been rich toward God?

The character of Christ cannot form in the heart of a man who is not willing to sacrifice the things of earth for the glory of heaven. The key to real sacrifice is believing that the glory of God is more important than anything you're giving up.

The ultimate example lives in you and dreams of the day He will share this same glory with you.

The Call to Suffer

The turning hour of a man's life is when he nobly accepts suffering for something greater than himself. This noble willingness makes men out of boys. It is responsible and mature. It is driven by a belief that some greater context encapsulates the suffering and gives it meaning. The cause becomes more significant than his suffering. So he endures it willingly, patiently, and aggressively.

By contrast, an unwillingness to suffer catastrophically stops a man's growth and precipitates regression.

1. What situations in your life have required suffering for the cause of Christ?

2. What did you learn in these situations of suffering?

📖 Good men don't have to suffer to keep their status in the world's eyes. "Don't rock the boat." "Just provide for your family and secure a good legacy." But for God's man, moving from good to great means embracing a turning hour in your spiritual journey where belief in Christ grows into a willingness to pay the price for that relationship and its purposes in your life. In its most basic sense, comfort and Christlikeness do not blend. 📖

3. Do you agree that it's possible to have a good reputation as a Christian man but still not be walking in full obedience to the Lord? Explain your answer.

📖 Opportunities to give up the comfort zone for the cause of Christ come up in every man's life. Individually, relationally, or emotionally, these divine moments must be seized in uncommon ways—ways that will not soothe or reassure your feelings and fears. These day-by-day choices will call your faith out on the carpet, expose it, and define it for years to come. 📖

4. What opportunities have you had to leave your comfort zone for the cause of Christ?

5. How did these experiences affect your faith?

Gain Through Pain

📖 Every form of pain endured for Christ is holy because you're aligned with Christ who suffered pain in every form. Christlikeness requires believing that God has authority over suffering. It is a mind-set that knows suffering achieves His dream of molding you into the image of Jesus. The Son suffered, and the adopted sons must be perfected like Him through the same sorrows, griefs, disappointments, and pains of earth. The Father refined Jesus into greatness and glory as our leader, and now it's His dream for you. Through your sufferings (chosen and circumstantial), you will grow into God's man. 📖

1. Why do you think suffering and pain are an important part of growing as a Christian?

📖 Life dishes out its worst, and it can crush you. But if your suffering is preempted with a deep and abiding trust in God's sovereign control of all things, you will prevail. "The reason my Father loves me is that I lay down my life—

only to take it up again. No one takes it from me, but I lay it down of my own accord. I have authority to lay it down and authority to take it up again" (John 10:17–18). The Man who said these confident and courageous words lives in you. 📖

2. Why did Jesus say, concerning His life, that He had the authority to lay it down and authority to take it up again?

3. What comfort and confidence do you have based on the truth that the same spirit that lived in Christ lives in you?

📖 Christ's suffering was never master over Him. And in a stunning blow to evil, Jesus proclaimed mastery over His suffering by choosing it out of love for the Father and acceptance of His cause. This was His turning hour as the Son of Man, choosing suffering as the path to greatness. This is His greatest imprint and highest example for followers seeking to be great.

And possibly even more unbelievable, you and I were the reason for this entire thing! "God, for whom and through whom everything was made, chose to bring many children into glory. And it was only right that he should make Jesus, through his suffering, a perfect leader, fit to bring them into their salvation. So now Jesus and the ones he makes holy have the same Father. That is why Jesus is not ashamed to call *them* his brothers and sisters" (Hebrews 2:10–11, NLT)....

Suffering pierces through the mystery of God and unites you to Him. More important, it qualifies you to lead in His kingdom work. 📖

4. Why was the suffering of Jesus the most stunning blow to evil on the earth?

5. Why does suffering qualify a Christian for kingdom work?

📖 No man wants to suffer. But God's man does not fear it because it unites him to his King. That is why we must lay down our own comforts, safeties, predictabilities, sureties, insecurities, fears, and prideful stances. Then we must pick up our crosses to experience God's ultimate vision for us. 📖

6. What are some ways in your day-to-day life that you pick up your cross?

📖 Trust in God and His purposes in the pain. God's man, don't let suffering disturb you. If you're suffering, it has been allowed by God in your life. Let it come. And know that it comes with great purpose in your life—to bring the greatest nobility possible—to become like our Brother, Jesus. 📖

7. How does knowing that God will not give you more than you can bear affect your response to suffering in your life?

📖 No leader in God's family has a greater connection to the cause of the kingdom than the man who has suffered to give it control in his own heart, relationships, and world.

What do you say to that? 📖

 **Dream Discipline**

Remember

For to me, to live is Christ and to die is gain. (Philippians 1:21)

Reflect

1. What do you think the apostle Paul meant by his words in Philippians?

2. Is there any sacrifice or suffering here on earth that will compare with the joy and satisfaction of spending eternity with God and all the saints?

Respond

Christians living in America and other developed nations often do not realize how much persecution their brothers and sisters in other parts of the world are suffering. This week take a few minutes to learn more about the suffering church. One way to do this is to visit the Open Doors Web site at www.opendoorsusa.org. You will find a plethora of information and realize you have much to pray about and be thankful for. Write some of your observations here.

Dream Debriefing (Man to Man)

Report to each other any answers to prayer or other memorable events from the previous week.

1. One topic in this week's study was suffering. Share with each other at least two instances where you have had to suffer.
2. Unpack together what you have learned from suffering. Has suffering made you a better man? How has God used suffering to make you a more mature disciple of Jesus?
3. In this session we also looked at how suffering on earth must be set in the context of God's great plans, which include rewards and everlasting joy in heaven. Discuss with one another the importance of heaven as you live through the challenges on earth?
4. Share personal requests and pray for each other.

Dream Interpretation (Small Group Discussion)

1. How difficult is it for you to wait for things or events—for the next meal, a new "toy," an evening alone with your wife, a game of golf, a fishing trip, or anything else you really want?

2. Why is waiting so tough?

3. Why is it important to learn how to wait patiently and well?

4. In this session of the workbook, we reviewed how waiting and other sacrifices here on earth are a necessary part of the Christian life. This statement appears in *Dream:* "The turning hour of a man's life is when he nobly accepts suffering for something greater than himself." What are some examples of noble suffering?

5. Have you had experiences where you had to suffer nobly? Share some of these stories.

6. The best model we have of how to endure suffering is Jesus. Together, make a list of incidents from Jesus's life where He suffered well.

7. In *Dream* it says, "Suffering for God's purposes unites us with Jesus." Has that been your experience? Share why this was the case.

Dream and Do

Here's what needs to happen before the next small group meeting:

1. Complete your personal study of session 4, which includes reading chapters 7 and 8 in *Dream.*

2. Meet with your accountability partner.

3. Accomplish the task you listed under Respond in the Dream Discipline section on page 72.

4. Record any of your observations in the Dream Journal.

Dream Journal

_____

_____

_____

_____

_____

_____

_____

_____

_____

_____

_____

_____

Father of dreams

This week's session is based on chapter 7, "My Father's Will," and chapter 8, "Locking Eyes," in Dream.

From the time I was a wee lad, I longed for my father's love and approval. I wanted to be tight with Dad. Didn't happen.

For years, my relationship with my dad was rocky. I have heard so many stories like mine, where the father-son scenario looked like this: busy, uninvolved dad…disappointed, hurting son…distant, hardened relationship.

Praise Jesus that in my dad's last years there was a spiritual breakthrough, and he and I really connected for the first time. I finally knew that Dad approved of me. (Read chapter 15 in *Dream* for the full story.)

I know that not every man will experience this connection with his earthly father. But there is another Father who promises to bond with *every one* of his boys—no exceptions. He waits with arms spread wide, a big grin on His face. Let's learn more about this.

✦ Dream Analysis

📖 Fathers project priorities and those priorities reflect their will. In this sense fathers become, almost by default, the driving forces of our lives. One friend told me that when his wife notices his dad's character coming out of him she calls him by his dad's name. It's not a positive experience for him, but he can't seem to help himself. The list of my father's will would look like this:

- respect (assumed by position)
- discipline
- hard work
- accountability
- authority
- self-sufficiency
- control (his)
- command (his)
- compliance
- punctuality

I saw my dad's will in each area. I felt it in the home. I adopted it as a priority. This alignment with his will was always good for him, sometimes good for me, and sometimes good for others. 📖

1. Related to the list of values and qualities you just read, how would you describe the will (priorities, passions, and desires) of your father? Write your own list here.

2. Which, if any, of your father's values and qualities drive you?

Jesus and Dad

Our relationship with our earthly father is critical—we are all hugely aware of that. But of far greater importance and impact is our relationship to the ultimate Father. We can learn many clues about the dynamics of this relationship from the life of our older Brother, Jesus.

Jesus Christ did reveal some aspects of how His Father and Son relationship worked with His Dad. He drew the analogy to the familiarity and relationship a shepherd has with his sheep. The sheep knew the voice, body language, whistle, and call of their shepherd.... Jesus possesses that kind of rare connection with the Father.

Over and over we see Jesus reference Their mutual commitment to executing a specific blueprint. He would say things like:

- "My food is to do the will of him who sent me" (John 4:34).
- "I do nothing on my own but speak just what the Father has taught me" (John 8:28).
- "These words you hear are not my own; they belong to the Father who sent me" (John 14:24).
- "For I have come down from heaven not to do my will but to do the will of him who sent me" (John 6:38).

Multiple statements like these reveal Jesus's unwavering commitment to God's purposes in the world. Jesus did not adopt His Father's will for selfish purposes, to garner His affection, avoid His anger, or experience a reward. For Jesus, it was a direct outcome of personally experiencing, seeing, and assigning importance to God's purposes as a willing agent of expression.

1. While Jesus was on earth, how do you think He maintained such tight focus on accomplishing the Father's purposes in the world?

2. How would you describe Jesus's mission on earth on behalf of the Father?

In the Gospels, Jesus presents a powerful picture of His Father as the creative mind and Himself the primary agent for its expression on earth. It is a dynamic relationship rooted in love, intimate knowledge, and a mutual commitment to accomplish very specific purposes. Before Jesus had healed one person, cast out one demon, or preached one message on the kingdom, an emphatic Father laid the foundation for His Son's fulfillment of His will by cementing their bond. It's a bond we will experience when we begin to venture successfully into the Father's will.

Here are three ways in which Jesus and God the Father were rooted in a superb relationship—the same relationship that is available to us with the Father.

Rooted in unconditional acceptance. "When all the people were being baptized, Jesus was baptized too. And as he was praying, heaven was opened and the

Holy Spirit descended on him in bodily form like a dove. And a voice came from heaven: 'You are my Son, whom I love; with you I am well pleased'" (Luke 3:21–22).

The relationship was solidly intact because of the expression and unique awareness of the Father's acceptance and affirmation of the Son, independent of his exploits.

Jesus hadn't done a thing at this point and *boom!*—a nuclear-sized expression of love on the part of the Father toward His Son.… With this type of love pulsating from His Father toward him, Jesus could afford to emotionally and relationally live for an audience of One and the will of One. He would not need the approval or acceptance of men. This made Him fearless in His focus and pursuit of the Father's priorities for His time on earth.

3. Have you ever received unconditional acceptance from another person? Remember, no one can perfectly do this!

4. In what ways do you live for the approval or acceptance of others?

5. Do you believe that God gives you unconditional acceptance? Why or why not?

📖 *Rooted in intimate knowledge.* "I tell you the truth, the Son can do nothing by himself; he can do only what he sees his Father doing, because whatever the Father does the Son also does. For the Father loves the Son and shows him all he does" (John 5:19–20).

This is a picture of mutual cooperation, the sharing of intimate knowledge, modeling, relationship, and love. There is a dependence on knowledge Jesus possessed of the Father that guided His own expression of His will on earth. He did not need to check it out with religious leaders of his day, modern thinkers, or the Roman authorities. He owned the Father's heart Himself. God's will had been plainly revealed and, therefore, would be plainly and authoritatively expressed in His life. Jesus's knowledge of the Father's heart kept His actions focused and pure in spite of His surroundings. 📖

6. What did Jesus mean when He said "the Son can do nothing by himself"?

7. When He was on earth, how do you think Jesus came to be so aware of what His Father's will was?

📖 *Rooted in mutual cooperation.* "Jesus said to them, 'My Father is always at his work to this very day, and I, too, am working'" (John 5:17).

The free exchange of feeling and thought between Jesus and God was a synergy of purpose the world had never seen. It was the Father & Son Redemption Co.: "Building the kingdom since 33 A.D." Because the Father loved the Son so deeply, He revealed His plans and purposes to Him, and the Son obediently carried them out. 📖

8. What plans and purposes of the Father has He revealed to you—and asked you to carry out?

📖 God's dream for you is to experience, as Jesus modeled, true fellowship and reciprocity with Him. Take a second and absorb that. Let it sink into your soul: your heavenly Father is seeking you out, His beloved son. 📖

You and Dad

📖 Astonishingly, the Good Shepherd laid down His life for His sheep to give you a chance for an intimate connection. "I am the good shepherd; I know my sheep and my sheep know me—just as the Father knows me and I know the Father—and I lay down my life for the sheep" (John 10:14–15).

No one knows you better than the Father, just as no one knew Jesus better than His Father.…

In fact, His desire is for you to experience the exact fullness of relationship with the Father that the original and only Son possesses. "Righteous Father, though the world does not know you, I know you, and they know that you have sent me. I have made you known to them, and will continue to make you known in order that the love you have for me may be in them and that I myself may be in them" (John 17:25–26).

The only Son wants you to experience and enjoy sonship with His Father. Have you fully embraced your adopting Father as Dad? 📖

1. How is your outlook on life affected by the fact that God knows you intimately?

2. In a day-to-day practical sense, how do you know that you know God well?

📖 God's man is ushered by Christ into this same exclusive relationship with the Father to possess and treasure a unique bond with the Father just as He did. "All things have been committed to me by my Father. No one knows the Son except the Father, and no one knows the Father except the Son and those to whom the Son chooses to reveal him" (Matthew 11:27).

That's you, God's man. 📖

3. What are the benefits of having an intimate relationship with God the Father?

4. How might you gain more from this insider opportunity to know God?

📖 Observe Jesus's prayer for you:

- "I in them and you in me. May they be brought to complete unity to let the world know that you sent me and have loved them even as you have loved me" (John 17:23). *Translation:* "Father, root them in your love by helping them see, accept, and embrace Your unconditional acceptance, the same acceptance you have for me. Then cut 'em loose!

- "That they may know you, the only true God, and Jesus Christ, whom you have sent" (John 17:3). *Translation:* "Give them an intimate, close-up knowledge of You through Me just like I have an intimate close-up knowledge of You. Help them model Your character, share Your heart and plans, and duplicate what they see in Our relationship."

- "As you sent me into the world, I have sent them into the world" (John 17:18). *Translation:* "They are going to work with us and commit to finishing what we started." 📖

5. Based on the bulleted passages listed here, what did Jesus pray to the Father about you?

6. What would you want to say in a prayer of response to Jesus's desires for you? As you are led by the Holy Spirit, touch on areas of repentance, praise, supplication, thanksgiving, and so on.

Because those who are led by the Spirit of God are sons of God. For you did not receive a spirit that makes you a slave again to fear, but you received the Spirit of sonship. And by him we cry, "Abba, Father." The Spirit himself testifies with our spirit that we are God's children. (Romans 8:14–16)

7. How does the Holy Spirit testify with your spirit that you are a son of God?

📖 God wants that special connection with you right now....

All fathers have dreams for what their sons could become. But in this case, there's an important difference. This Father can't disappoint. There are no haunting thoughts or demons of character that can sabotage His deepest wishes and visions for your life. Nothing can ever prevent Him from being the prime example of what He wants you to become. 📖

The Family Business

Now that our older Brother has returned to heaven and is sitting at the right hand of the Father (see 1 Peter 3:21–22), it's our turn to run the family business. We are to be what is called "little Christs" in our loyalty and obedience to our Father.

📖 Christlikeness is all about sonship with the Father. 📖

📖 In your journey to realize God's dream for your life, God's will must be at the forefront of your mind. What is God's will? It's directly reflected in the character of Christ. In Jesus, we see an aggressive freedom to pursue, articulate, and accept His Father's will. In his connection to the Father's will, God's man sees it, feels it, adopts it, integrates it, and is individually motivated to pursue it. 📖

1. How would you describe the Father's will for you? Be as specific as possible.

📖 God's dream for you is to be a doer of the Father's will. That's as opposed to being a:

- discusser of His will
- debater of His will
- deconstructor of His will
- dissector of His will
- deflector of His will
- delayer of His will
- dealmaker of His will
- doubter of His will

This life of doing the Father's will is a combination of promise and persecution, blessing and suffering.... The best news is that Jesus Christ accepts all men into His brotherhood and all men can begin today to do the one thing that distinguishes a brother of Christ: the will of the Father. 📖

2. How have you been blessed while doing the will of the Father?

📖 His dream is to be the creative force in your life, for you to be an agent of His expression, and to give you the active power to pull this off through the Holy Spirit.... This offer is lost on many men of faith. They don't get it, don't see it, don't experience God's anointing and adoption upon their lives as His sons. In other words, they miss the dream. 📖

3. Explain why you agree or disagree that many men don't experience God's anointing and adoption as His sons.

📖 Only a true dad's heart could say, "How gladly would I treat you like sons and give you a desirable land, the most beautiful inheritance of any nation. I thought you would call me 'Father' and not turn away from following me" (Jeremiah 3:19).... Maybe this is beyond what we can understand, but maybe it was that the thought of rejection was impossible, even for God. 📖

4. How might you be a better son to your Father in heaven?

📖 Any man who reacts to God's will out of a crushing fear of losing His favor or stirring His anger inevitably ends up resigning, resenting, or resisting His will. Fear and mixed motives always mess up a good thing....

Becoming like Christ means learning how to live as a son, how to trust your Father so intuitively and implicitly that conscious communication gives way to an internalized, symbiotic sonship. You can go from guessing to knowing what He is feeling and respond to that as your guiding force. You can know His desires as His son, know the look in His eyes, the nod of His head. 📖

5. What will it take for you to have such a tight relationship with your Father God that you know what He is feeling?

📖 Yes, you can be this close. In God's dream, you belong to Him. Consider this belonging to be the distinction between vocational worship and relational son-ship. One flow is time and people driven. The other flow is presence and Father driven. One is a public process of mutual partnership and investment in a co-mission. The other is a masculine dance of soul and knowledge between Father and follower. According to the Scriptures, both of these dynamic relationships are meaning oriented, but only one is personal, extending into the realm of a family tie that binds closer than all others. 📖

Dream Discipline

Remember

For you did not receive a spirit that makes you a slave again to fear, but you received the Spirit of sonship. And by him we cry out, "Abba, Father." (Romans 8:15)

Reflect

1. In writing these words to the Christians at Rome, why do you think Paul contrasted slavery and sonship to describe the state of the believer?

2. What does having the Spirit of sonship mean in your life?

Respond

This week, make a list of the advantages available to you because you are a son of the Father.

📓 Dream Debriefing (Man to Man)

Open in prayer. Take turns giving a summary of your relationship with your earthly father. Is it good? Not so good?

1. Ask each other, "When you were growing up, how did your earthly father mirror the character qualities of your heavenly Father? How did he not mirror the qualities of your heavenly Father?

2. Regardless of the quality of experience with your dads, take turns offering a prayer of thanksgiving for them.

〜 Dream Interpretation (Small Group Discussion)

1. How would you describe your relationship with your earthly father?
2. Does your earthly father want to get to know you and spend time with you?
3. What instances do you recall from the New Testament that reveal Jesus's ardent pursuit of the Father's will?
4. Describe what it means to know that God the Father desires to relate to you as a son just like He related to His other Son, Jesus?
5. How is your outlook on life affected by the fact that God knows you intimately?
6. How can you go about better cementing your bond with God the Father?
7. As a group, make a list of the advantages of being God's son.

☀ Dream and Do

Here's what needs to happen before the next small group meeting:

1. Complete your personal study of session 5, which includes reading chapters 9, 10, and 11 in *Dream*.
2. Meet with your accountability partner.
3. Accomplish the task you listed under Respond in the Dream Discipline section on page 89.
4. Record any of your observations in the Dream Journal.

 **Dream Journal**

_____

_____

_____

_____

_____

_____

_____

_____

_____

_____

_____

_____

man after His heart

This week's session is based on chapter 9, "Aspirin with Skin," chapter 10, "Seeing Past," and chapter 11, "Velvet Touch," in Dream.

Only God really knows what is happening in a person's heart.

I learned this repeatedly when I worked in the mental health field. Thousands of individual assessments with hurting people showed me that the bigger the song-and-dance on the outside, the bigger the hurt on the inside. It doesn't matter if it's a teenager dressed in all black or a woman wearing too much makeup and too few clothes; these people are crying out for attention and affirmation.

Such behavior didn't surprise Jesus. He once said that He knew exactly what was in the heart of man (see Luke 6:45) and knew exactly how to respond. Jesus looked flawed people in the eye with a steady gaze of acceptance and love. In this He was just representing what He had learned from His Father about compassion, tenderness, and love for hurting men and women.

Now that we represent Jesus on this hurting planet, we have the opportunity to understand and help people in the same way. Let's learn from our older Brother how to become a God's man after the Father's own heart.

✦ Dream Analysis

📖 We are floating in an ocean of friends and acquaintances, co-workers, church fellowships, and tons of fraternities of men that only see our tips. These are the emotional truths men are keeping below the surface 24/7, and no one knows how influential these matters are to his life. The tragedy is that these problems lurking below produce a plethora of negative emotions. And left to our own devices, we will translate those emotions into unhealthy responses. These powerful feelings are the jagged edges that will shipwreck families, faith, and futures.

What's incredible is that male cultures worldwide are trained to accept just the tip, the visible surface of men, at the expense of the real substance of his life. We take what people say at face value, ask inch-deep questions and gladly rubber stamp an answer....

Jesus was simply not interested in the show, the presentation, or the justified or unjustified surface emotions of people. He had no taste for the symptoms; He went after the root. His mission was to enter and redeem hearts, not to respond to disguises, diversions, or denial. His modus operandi was based on what He knew about people: that we're all icebergs with deeper spiritual dramas unfolding below the waterline. The difference is that He would go there. He would do a heart scan rather than a behavioral assessment.... What did He see?

- hurts
- fears
- insecurities
- sin
- mixed motives
- lust

- wounds
- abandonment
- shame
- pride
- loss
- negative emotions à la carte 📖

1. What experiences have you had in learning that a friend or acquaintance had a lot going on below the surface?

2. What issues do you find that people hide beneath the surface?

📖 We can't act so surprised when a brother in our close-knit community does something that we term as scandal. How can we express shock at men's behavior when, if we're honest, there's no true relational basis there? What personal knowledge allows us to be shocked? Afterward, comments about The Scandal stem from a perceived image based on wafer-thin interactions like passing at the mailbox. 📖

3. Are relationships in your church superficial? Why do you say this?

📖 Jesus was not a man who accepted anybody's tip. He always worked to get below the waterline and help people accept the real issues. They were the issues preventing them from experiencing His best for their lives. If you want to be God's man and live out the character of the God-Man, you can't accept tips any longer either. 📖

What Jesus Did

📖 [Jesus] made it a habit to connect with the sexually immoral, physically unclean, and ethnically impure.…

Jesus did not blend with contemporary religious expression simply because He made His grace available to all. To be this way, He could not be codependent with culture, racial caricature, tradition, or the pseudoholy practices of exclusion. To deliver God's grace on earth, the criteria was this: honest need. When He found this, He would jump in the boat and make it over to that person's shore. "Jesus unplugged" is a story of grace in motion—dangerously attractive, inviting, and controversial. And God's dream for us is that we be the same.…

Jesus would intentionally go to where real pain, pride, or paranoia existed, because He knew that was where the potential for real spiritual change existed. 📖

1. List some encounters where Jesus connected with people who were outcasts or not a part of the in crowd.

2. Why are people so eager to hide what's really going on inside them?

3. Why was Jesus so intent on dealing with the "below the waterline" issues of the people He encountered?

The good news is that He wants to give you His ability to see those issues and help you be motivated to use that ability. This is real love. True discernment of people without Christ-centered love is not possible. Any other way and you have an agenda.

This is nonnegotiable in following Jesus's footsteps and becoming a good spiritual cardiologist. "And this is my prayer: that your love may abound more and more in knowledge and depth of insight, so that you may be able to discern what is best and may be pure and blameless until the day of Christ, filled with the fruit of righteousness that comes through Jesus Christ—to the glory and praise of God" (Philippians 1:9–11).

4. Describe your ability to discern what is really going on with other people?

5. Have you ever felt someone had less-than-pure motives or an agenda in wanting to know more about your interior life? If yes, how did that feel?

📖 Compassion gladdens the hearts of those who travel the road of pain.... Every day that Jesus walked the earth there were plenty of battles being fought— physical, emotional, political, relational, and psychological—into which His compassion found a place. Without compassion, Jesus could not have met the demands of the realities He came to address. And as His agent and ambassador, neither can you. His example did not presume compassion alone could eliminate evil entirely, but He could mitigate it, engage and resist it while on earth.

That's what made Jesus, Jesus. It's what makes God's man, God's man. 📖

6. How might you become a more compassionate person?

📖 History for each of us will culminate in a cosmic act of compassion on God's part. "He will wipe every tear from their eyes. There will be no more death or mourning or crying or pain" (Revelation 21:4). God's compassion triumphs in heaven, alleviating our losses, suffering, and pain. The main reason we cannot shake off the needs of others is because God never shakes ours off! 📖

Acquiring the Father's Heart

Oh, how I want to be more able like Jesus to minister to the hurting hearts that I encounter every day! I long to have the compassionate heart of my heavenly Father beating inside my chest.

📖 When the Bible says, "Your attitude should be the same as that of Christ Jesus," you can't miss His character of compassion (Philippians 2:5). If His dream for us is Christ Himself, then God looks at you and sees that there is nothing so basic to your identity as compassion....

Compassion lets the world know you are free to be God's man.... God's dream for you is that you would be equally strong and secure in Him so that the compassion of Christ could flow freely to those who need your touch. Compassion established Jesus as a God pleaser versus a man pleaser. Our freedom to touch and meet needs is always a reflection of our identity. 📖

1. How do you think we develop a strong and secure identity in Christ?

2. Do you consider yourself more of a man pleaser or a God pleaser? Explain your answer.

3. What does it look like for you to live for an audience of One?

📖 Slowly I am coming to a new definition of manhood, one rooted in tenderness as a sign of spiritual toughness. I am beginning to feel the truth that the best parts of my life will be the forgotten acts of compassion that were remembered by God. I am learning that compassion trumps condemnation every time and that practical empathy provides needed emotional shade to the sun-baked and weary soul—a comfort, a relief, a pause that allows that person to forget their pain and find hope again.

Jesus's tendency toward tenderness and comforting others in pain is well documented. His kindness never weakened His stamina or softened His fiber— it just made Him stand out more as a leader. We see Him move about freely in extending compassion, but we don't see someone who met every single need. What we do see is a man moved by need who allows the need to move Him. 📖

4. List some of the "insignificant," small acts of compassion others have done for you. Thank God for the people who blessed you with these expressions of kindness.

Let's face it. Extending the compassion of Jesus stretches us. Why is it so difficult sometimes?

   📖 Inability to be tender is fear—of man, of appearances, or of reality, which hides an even deeper fear of responsibility....

But [intimacy is] reachable because, "I can do everything through him who gives me strength" (Philippians 4:13). And He says that His character, which includes recognizing pain and acting with compassion, can be formed in me.

What would show the world that a man's heart is free to respond to the Holy Spirit? Answer: tenderness. 📖

5. Do you consider yourself a tender person? Why or why not?

6. What do you think causes your failure to show compassion at times?

   📖 Maybe you, like me, have not graduated from the school of compassion. I actually trained myself not to feel. To survive as young man, I fought the feelings battle. It's become a life habit. But I am relearning how to be tender, to be fearless in Christ. And I'm discovering that this compassion and tenderness costs me very little. Yet it accomplishes so much in the lives of others when I simply have the courage to act on it in faith. This keeps my willingness to risk high. 📖

Spreading Grace

📖 Why is it that so much is said about grace while so few of us give it away? A simple presence, an embrace and acceptance moves the prodigals back in the right direction. Yet instead of having a soft spot for sinners, we're terrified of them. Generally, the message we send is that the saints don't need the sinners. It's a good thing Jesus didn't feel the same. "The Son of Man came eating and drinking, and they say, 'Here is a glutton and a drunkard, a friend of tax collectors and "sinners" ' " (Matthew 11:19)....

"The Word became flesh and made his dwelling among us. We have seen his glory, the glory of the One and Only, who came from the Father, full of grace and truth" (John 1:14). Jesus—the Word in the flesh—was the ambassador of God's grace. We cannot compartmentalize this most radical and transforming aspect of Jesus's character. We can't separate it from our journey as God's man. 📖

1. How would you describe your communication with non-Christians?

2. What have you done for others that has shown grace?

3. In what ways might you become a more effective ambassador of God's grace?

I don't know who makes it onto your private quarantine list, maybe a homosexual co-worker, an obese neighbor, an alcoholic uncle, your "out there" son-in-law, but just think of someone you shy away from. Why are you afraid? Why do they give you a fever emotionally? How has God called you to relate to them?

4. Who are the people in your life that you find hard to love?

This spiritual skill also implies a clear ability to help others understand what really matters in life in order to integrate those core values into our lives. Our task as God's men in connecting with others is to be guided by love and an ability to see the important stuff, to discern. "What's that?" you ask. It means you care enough to know their heart issues and you're good at asking questions that connect to the heart. The biggies would be:

- family issues, past and present
- family losses
- other relationships
- personal core struggles and fears
- biggest hurts
- personality and wiring

See? It's not a long list. From the first century to the new millennium, people's core issues have not changed. 📖

5. Do you agree with the core heart issue list (quoted just previously), or would you add some items of your own?

📖 When you care enough to search out the main issues of someone's heart, you become privy to who that person really is.... Like Jesus, you're called to train your recognition of the differences between appearances and reality, between public images and private struggles, between anger and hurt, pride and fear. God's man, like the God-Man, is ever growing in his abilities to scan for good and bad intentions, right and wrong agendas, healthy and unhealthy spiritual patterns, and the vital issues behind people's words, behaviors, and thoughts. 📖

6. On a 1 (low) to 10 (high) scale, how would you rate your abilities on the following:
    _____ understanding what might be bugging someone who is visibly upset
    _____ discerning when another person has a concealed agenda
    _____ determining if a person is faking spiritual integrity

7. Based on your answers to the previous question, in what areas do you need more instruction on discerning the true state of another person's heart?

📖 Compassion is not about me but about fighting for others. Now *that* I connect with. I love helping people fight their unseen battles in the name of Jesus. But to do that, I have to develop discernment and sensitivity to see when the battle is raging. I need those eyes to see. I learn the most by studying Jesus, getting a feel for His rhythm, and recognizing that emotionally tough situations are the exact moments when He's calling me to care....

If you are like me, you have to let go of your fears and let Jesus take over. I am not a radical, go-out-of-my-way connector, especially with people not like me. I much prefer sanitized and tidy. But that's not going to cut it. I must study Him, watch Him, and seek to agent His grace. When I look closely at the Gospels, I'm convicted, because what I see is that nothing stopped the God-Man from affirming and accepting excluded people. He went to them and they went to Him. In every case, grace and people collided beautifully.

I want the excluded to feel Him when they collide with me. 📖

8. What experiences have you had helping others fight their unseen battles in the name of Jesus?

9. In what situations have others shown you compassion in fighting your unseen battles?

 The great news is that we have the best teacher in the universe. [Jesus] shows us the way into the heart. He prompts us as we study others. We can see His mind in the Scriptures, dialogue with Him, ask Him for discernment, listen for His voice, and respond to His direction. The skill comes as we seek to help the lost find their way to Him and ultimately to find their healing in Him....

In this sense, the dream is simple: be moved and move.

Dream Discipline

Remember

Greater love has no one than this, that he lay down his life for his friends. (John 15:13)

Reflect

1. Why is laying down your life for a friend the greatest kind of love?

2. List the people who have shown you sacrificial love. State briefly how they laid down their lives to love you.

Respond

During the next few days, visit, call, e-mail, or write one of the people you listed and tell him or her how much you appreciate the sacrificial love he or she gave. Describe what you said and/or how that conversation went.

 **Dream Debriefing (Man to Man)**

Take turns catching up on what has happened to each of you this past week.

1. Since you are accountability brothers, take turns commenting on any below-the-waterline issues that need exposure.

2. Compassion was a theme of this session. Ask each other, "How easy or hard is it for you to show kindness to others?"

3. Share prayer requests. In particular, pray for one another about any deeper personal issues revealed in your time together.

 Dream Interpretation (Small Group Discussion)

1. This workbook session discussed the idea that people are like icebergs: there's much more below the surface than above. Ask the group, "Has it been your experience that people conceal a lot about themselves?"

2. Why do people do that?

3. Why was Jesus so effective at learning what was below the surface with the people He met?

4. What can we do to help other people expose harmful secrets so God can heal the wounds? How can we be more transparent ourselves?

5. Sometimes certain kinds of people are more difficult to love. Who do you have difficulty loving?

6. What are some things we can do that will give us a greater heart of compassion for others in need?

☼ Dream and Do

Here's what needs to happen before the next small group meeting:

1. Complete your personal study of session 6, which includes reading chapter 12 in *Dream*.

2. Meet with your accountability partner.

3. Accomplish the task you listed under Respond in the Dream Discipline section on page 109.

4. Record any of your observations in the Dream Journal.

 **Dream Journal**

_____

_____

_____

_____

_____

_____

_____

_____

reality check

This week's session is based on chapter 12, "Bullish on Reality," in Dream.

One of God's dreams for us is that we will always stay in touch with reality. That means that as God's men here on kingdom assignment, our eyes are clear, our hearts are clean, and our feet are planted firmly on the Rock. Our heads are not in the clouds.

This is a tall order: maintaining a consistent attachment to reality. Frankly, only one person has ever completely pulled this off: our older Brother, Jesus. He never lost His perspective on what was true. He saw the reality of earth and its inhabitants and never blinked. He was not distracted by Satan's deceptions and the games people play, so Jesus could deliver real compassion and solutions for the dilemmas of humanity. His ability to simultaneously face truth and deliver grace has never been matched.

And guess what: God expects the same performance from you and me! No pressure, huh?

In fact, we do have the ability because of the indwelling of the Holy Spirit to face reality and influence people as Jesus did. How can we pull that off? It's time for a reality check.

 Dream Analysis

Here's how the dictionary defines *reality:* "Not the way we wish things to be, nor the way they appear, but the way things actually are." Ouch! That definition makes me wonder, *Am I really in touch with reality?*

> 📖 Being God's man means being a man whose character is centered in the true reality. *Versus what?* you ask. Versus being a man centered on appearances. Perceptions. Rationalizations. Deceits. Fantasies. Self-deceptions and all other shades of unreality. Christlikeness is measured by a consistent acceptance of reality—especially when it hurts. How do I know? Because this is the essence of the God-Man. The velvet touch of His grace is seamlessly paired with this indestructible commitment to truth. They are the two parts of His character that bring healing and health to all He touches…. Grace feels like a comfortable hug. Truth feels like a swift slap to the backside.
>
> Yet both show love. 📖

1. Why do you think people find it difficult to accept reality?

📖 I see this reality fudging going on all the time in men's ministry, especially when husbands have grown deeply afraid of reality and lead their wives to believe some sort of falsehood. I see it in pastors unwilling to share their dark sides of struggle with temptation because of the pedestal effect—when the pressure of popularity puts them in a prison of pomposity and self-preservation. I see it when men are unable to accept the brutal facts surrounding lust and fantasy and its lasting impact on relationships. I see it in superficial male relationships—guys bleeding right in front in their buddies' eyes.…

All of this emotional cloak and dagger, fear and pride, denial and neglect turns Jesus's stomach and breaks His heart. 📖

2. How would you describe reality fudging by men?

3. Why do men struggle to have authentic relationships with each other?

4. In what areas of your life are you tempted to put on the mask and adjust your perceived image?

📖 "This is the crisis we're in: God-light streamed into the world, but men and women everywhere ran for the darkness. They went for the darkness because they were not really interested in pleasing God. Everyone who makes a practice of doing evil, addicted to denial and illusion, hates God-light and won't come near it, fearing a painful exposure. But anyone working and living in truth and reality welcomes God-light so the work can be seen for the God-work it is" (John 3:19–21, MSG).

This is what new birth as a man will look and feel like. The light of Christ shines into the secret places and exposes realities in our lives, the gaps He would like to help us fill. A full exposure to His light in our lives is the bright kind, leaving no corner unilluminated and leaving us exposed morally, emotionally, relationally, and spiritually. 📖

5. How have you welcomed—or not welcomed—God's light streaming into the concealed parts of your life?

6. Take a moment and thank God for sending His light into your life. This is really good news! We don't have to fear reality.

Get Real

We have no choice. If we want to hang out with Jesus, we'd better get in touch with reality. If you don't believe this, follow the reality story line in the Gospels. Some examples? Did the disciples, the Roman centurion with the sick daughter, the Samaritan woman at the well, the rich young ruler, the Pharisees, or Pilate really doubt that Jesus was devoted to reality?

📖 Jesus was big on reality.

Sounds cliché, but when you study Him, the words He speaks, and His interactions with men, you see that He wanted people to possess the truth no matter the cost.

In this sense I am so unlike Him. I lie naturally. I cover up naturally. I don't want people to be mad at me. I want to be accepted. I want people to feel good. I don't want to hurt others. My character can disintegrate in these hard realities—it gets exposed. My courage to face, speak, live out, and integrate the whole truth about my flaws is difficult without His spine in me, holding me up. 📖

1. How difficult is it for people to uncover their thoughts? Explain your answer.

2. If you had to prove you are an honest person, what evidence would you present?

📖 Accept reality. Work with Jesus. Stop running....

Surrender to the Master Craftsman's loving pursuit of truth for us so He can finish His shaping work....

Jesus confronts all men with the facts, because anything less on His side makes Him a fraud and makes you not a brother....

To be like Christ, the gloves must come off. It's time to see, engage, and inter-act with what *is,* not what you wish it was. It takes a man-sized courage to live in truth and reality—you must be open to personal transformation. 📖

3. On a scale of 1 to 10, with 1 meaning, *I am barely in touch with reality,* and 10 meaning, *I am in touch with reality most of the time,* how do you rate your attach-ment to reality?

4. What does your rating suggest you need to do to improve as a God's man in the area of reality?

Downloading Authenticity

📖 Jesus, being the embodiment of all truth, knew the consequences of deceit with precise intuition. That's why God's dream for us to be like Christ includes the trait of authenticity—to permit reality and truth to guide our actions. 📖

I have prepared a list of scriptures that show how Jesus taught how we should integrate reality into real life. Your answers to the questions will help you gauge the level of your own authenticity.

📖 *Reality and temptation.* "If your hand causes you to sin, cut it off. It is better for you to enter life maimed than with two hands to go into hell" (Mark 9:43). The hard truth: amputate sin like a cancer. Be ruthless with it and unapologetic. If you don't, it will metastasize to come back, fester, and eventually kill you. That's a certainty. 📖

1. Can you recall a time when you did not amputate sin and that decision came back to haunt you?

📖 *Reality and God's commands.* "Why do you call me, 'Lord, Lord,' and do not what I say?" (Luke 6:46). The hard truth: spiritual actions speak far louder than words. They are the ultimate marker of spiritual integrity. If you love someone, you seek alignment of your life to their priorities. 📖

2. List the areas of your life where you find obedience difficult.

📖 *Reality and spiritual deception.* "You have heard that it was said, 'Do not commit adultery.' But I tell you that anyone who looks at a woman lustfully has already committed adultery with her in his heart" (Matthew 5:27–28). The hard truth: thoughts, motives, and intentions reveal who we really are, and behaviors only confirm it. The tip of the iceberg is what people see. The mass below the waterline is what God sees. 📖

3. The problem with deception is that it's deceptive! Are there areas in your life where you might be more prone to Satan's lies?

📖 *Reality and expectations.* "I have told you these things, so that in me you may have peace. In this world you will have trouble, but take heart! I have overcome the world" (John 16:33). The hard truth: earth is not heaven; we should expect loss and grief. Yet we should anticipate God's redeeming our grief and fulfilling His purpose in it. Though full redemption of suffering may not come in this lifetime, earth's worst cannot escape God's best. 📖

4. In what areas of your life do you struggle most with unrealistic expectations?

📖 *Reality and spiritual practice.* "You hypocrites! Isaiah was right when he prophesied about you: 'These people honor me with their lips, but their hearts are far from me.'" (Matthew 15:7–8). The hard truth: the motions might be right, but if the motivations are out of alignment, you might as well drop the charade. Playing church is playing with fire. 📖

5. We all struggle to align our internal and external realities. Where are you most tempted to play the hypocrite?

📖 *Reality and loss.* "When Jesus saw her weeping, and the Jews who had come along with her also weeping, he was deeply moved in spirit and troubled. 'Where have you laid him?' he asked. 'Come and see, Lord,' they replied. Jesus wept"

(John 11:33–35). The hard truth: we are made to feel pain, not brush it off as someone else's misery. Jesus did not deny or try to fix the real loss of others in the moment. He experienced and connected with it. Anything less is out of touch with reality. 📖

6. What has been your greatest experience of pain?

7. What did you learn about God and His faithfulness through this pain experience?

📖 *Reality and emotional isolation.* "Come to me, all who are weary and burdened, and I will give you rest" (Matthew 11:28). The hard truth: there is no such thing as emotionally satisfying self-sufficiency. There is only One with unlimited emotional resources—and you are not Him. 📖

8. How are you doing with letting the Lord Jesus bear your burdens?

Reality and persecution. " 'No servant is greater than his master.' If they perse-cuted me, they will persecute you" (John 15:20). The hard truth: a relationship with Jesus Christ involves suffering. Sign me up!

9. Have you ever experienced persecution because of your faith? Do you expect you will experience persecution in the future?

Reality and dysfunction. " 'Martha, Martha,' the Lord answered, 'you are wor-ried and upset about many things, but only one thing is needed. Mary has cho-sen what is better, and it will not be taken away from her' " (Luke 10:41–42). The hard truth: He accepts us as we are but loves us too much to leave us the way we are. Oh man, that's awkward, but it's a necessary part of reality and loving someone to health.

10. In the Mary and Martha story, what was the "better" that Mary chose (see the whole story in Luke 10:38–42).

11. In your relationship with Christ, how successful have you been in choosing what is better? Explain your answer.

📖 *Reality and secrets.* " 'Go, call your husband and come back.' 'I have no husband,' she replied. Jesus said to her, 'You are right when you say you have no husband. The fact is, you have had five husbands, and the man you now have is not your husband. What you have just said is quite true' " (John 4:16–18). The hard truth: Jesus has seen our movie—every frame. Nothing is lost in translation here. Jesus knows all the facts about our dark spaces. That is either terrifying or quite relieving. Now we don't have to pretend or hide anything. It's for us, not Him. 📖

12. What secrets, if any, are you trying to hide from Jesus?

📖 *Reality and eternity.* "In my Father's house are many rooms; if it were not so, I would have told you. I am going there to prepare a place for you" (John 14:2). The wonderful truth: we are never going to be separated—ever! This is the best reality of all. 📖

13. This is a good time for prayer. Confess anything that needs correction. Thank God for His forgiveness. Praise Him for the reality of an incredible life with Him after this earthly life is completed.

The hard part? Admitting your identity and your energies may have been partially misplaced. But you have the opportunity today to become more like Christ—a man who doesn't have to create a world of unreality to make himself feel better or more secure.

Reality Check

After all this analysis, are there signposts that help us determine that our character is becoming more like Christ's—more rooted in truth and reality?

Are you there yet? Or are you still selective about the reality you accept? What are you not able to confront yet? What is the big, fat hairy elephant in the space of your life? Is God big enough to handle your truth? Does He have enough love to cover it? Does He have enough power and purpose to transform it? These are the questions which lead you to be like Christ—putting you in touch with reality and truth, versus cultivating more fantasy. One life is authentic and feels real. The other is synthetic and feels superficial.

1. Any big, fat hairy elephants still lounging about in your life? If so, how might you pick up your elephant gun and go on safari?

How does God's man know his character is becoming more like Christ's—more rooted in truth, in reality? For God's man it is the difference between the Old You and the New You—the Christ-formed one. The Christ-led man negotiates and lives in reality well. He is able to speak the truth, acknowledge the truth in a situation, and encourage others to face reality with a truthful perspective. He's learned that the emotionally convenient and comfortable response is often the misleading one. He is guided by the Holy Spirit's strong leadership, and finds truth in reality. When this happens, plenty more good stuff comes about in God's man. He:

- accepts responsibility and evaluates his shortcomings
- seeks constructive feedback from others and embraces consequences
- acknowledges and deals with negative emotions versus swallowing them
- makes the hard (and better) call early
- doesn't hide from losses and hurts, but grieves them
- stops blaming others to cover for his mistakes
- stops seeking affirmation to compensate for insecurity
- speaks up with others, to them, and for them when the Holy Spirit prompts

2. Review the bulleted list. How are you doing as a reality seeker? Note areas where you want God's help in making improvements.

The Real Deal

📖 When I take bold steps toward painful realities, I know it is Jesus in me and not myself. How do I know? First, because it's not my natural pattern. I prefer comfort. I prefer safe fantasy. Second, because Jesus did not spin the facts when there was a risk of loss or a potentially negative consequence. In fact, he leaned in harder when there was a risk of people believing fantasies. Did this make Jesus a wet rag? Sometimes. No one likes their parade rained on. But when our parade gets out of control, the truth of our circumstances can be a refreshing rain....

What does authenticity feel like? Every "aha" moment, every, "Whoa, that's deep!" and every, "*Now* I see," is the result of His work in your life. Jesus Christ takes full credit for all truth. 📖

1. As a result of the reality check you have taken in this lesson, are there any "aha" bursts of new understanding you want to list here?

God's purpose in getting us more in touch with reality is not just so we can be more whole ourselves—as helpful as that is. No, He has something even more important in mind. When we understand reality, then we can truly minister as Christ would to the needs and hurts of others. Seeing reality opens the door to expression of deep compassion.

 **Dream Discipline**

Remember

> When Jesus spoke again to the people, he said, "I am the light of the world. Whoever follows me will never walk in darkness, but will have the light of life." (John 8:12)

Reflect

1. Why is Jesus the light of the world?

2. What areas of your life could use some of Jesus's light?

Respond

Jesus said, "Let your light shine before men, that they may see your good deeds and praise your Father in heaven" (Matthew 5:16). This week, connect with someone who could use the illumination and warmth of Jesus's light: buy a lunch, cut a yard, wash a car, send a card. Get creative! Describe what you did here.

Dream Debriefing (Man to Man)

Catch up on what's been going on since you last met.

1. Facing reality in our lives can be tough. Share with each other any spots where swallowing reality is a struggle—relationships, family, job, church, walk with God, health, and so on.
2. Pray for each other, asking God for His help in facing the real issues of your life with integrity, persistence, and strength.

 **Dream Interpretation (Small Group Discussion)**

1. Our study this session deals with the topic of reality. Men are often accused of disguising what is going on inside of them. Do you agree that this is true? Why or why not?

2. Why is it difficult at times to admit to others that there is a worry, weakness, inadequacy, or similar challenge we are concealing?

3. What are some of the reasons men might give for not sharing their real issues with others?

4. Jesus said that "the truth will set you free" (John 8:32). What happens when something hidden in our lives is brought into the open?

5. In our fast-paced, self-sufficient age, many men have difficulty finding even one good guy friend. Ask the men in the group how they go about developing and maintaining such relationships. Is anyone having trouble making such a connection?

6. The Bible advises "confess your sins to each other" (James 5:16) and that "whoever confesses and renounces [his sins] finds mercy" (Proverbs 28:13). What advantages might come from men getting real and confessing their sins to each other?

Dream and Do

Here's what needs to happen before the next small group meeting:

1. Complete your personal study of session 7, which includes reading chapter 13 in *Dream*.

2. Meet with your accountability partner.

3. Accomplish the task you listed under Respond in the Dream Discipline section on page 126.

4. Record any of your observations in the Dream Journal.

 **Dream Journal**

_____

_____

_____

_____

_____

_____

_____

_____

soldiers fit for battle

This week's session is based on chapter 13, "Soldier of Heaven," in Dream.

At the beginning of the twenty-first century, America is at war—a conflict called the war on terror.

Although the terrorists had bombed and attacked before, for most Americans the war really began in a dramatic way on the morning of September 11, 2001, when two planes crashed into the twin towers in New York City. Much like the morning at Pearl Harbor, 9/11 will be remembered as a day of infamy.

As horrifying as the war waged by terrorists is, there is another war on earth with exponentially greater consequences: the war against the kingdom of God. This conflict has raged for centuries between satanic terrorists against God's army. And with no possibility of a peace declaration, the casualties mount.

Whether you like it or not, you, my brother, are a soldier in this war. The front line of battle runs right through your heart and mind. The enemy's suicide bombers are parked outside your door. A terrorist may live in the condo next door or be making calls from the next cubicle. You better lock and load—the air raid sirens are blaring.

The good news is that if you are a soldier in Christ's battalion, ultimate victory is assured. But in the meantime, there's a mop-up operation underway. Our side is under vicious attack, and your brothers and sisters are getting hit.

How are you going to respond, trooper?

 **Dream Analysis**

The very act of identification with Jesus Christ means one irrefutable thing for you—you are the enemy of hell....

As stunning as a full-scale declaration of war among nations would be, as lamentable and grievous as the costs, this war, our war, engenders cosmic consequences that dwarf every hell of every war ever fought....

As a soldier of heaven...your faith is a cosmic crusade with Christ leading the charge, His eyes fixed, His blade drawn. The Rider, calling to His men, "Swords to the ready!"

1. Do you typically view yourself as a soldier of heaven? Why or why not?

2. What evidence in your life indicates that you are in a vicious spiritual battle?

For our struggle is not against flesh and blood, but against the rulers, against the authorities, against the powers of this dark world and against the spiritual forces of evil in the heavenly realms. (Ephesians 6:12)

📖 There are eager forces working hard to thwart God's work. They may be unseen, but they desperately want control and power over us. Jesus Christ has given us the intelligence and tools to fight the forces that oppose us....

There is no such thing as peaceful coexistence on this one. Instead there will be violent campaigns of spiritual warfare and forceful men prosecuting them.

Are satanic forces and human beings presently cooperating to prosecute evil against God's Son and followers? Yes. That is the unpolluted reality, my brother. 📖

3. How might your interaction with people change because you know that your struggles are not against flesh and blood but instead against powers of this dark world and against the spiritual forces of evil?

4. List examples from your life now that reveal the spiritual war between God and Satan.

📖 Jesus came to wage spiritual battle and win back His hostages from the hand of the Enemy. It's all Him. It's His war. He declared a jihad against Satan and sin. This is His battle and when it comes to blows, there is real blood—lots of it. 📖

5. List some examples from Christ's life that indicate He was involved in a spiritual war.

6. What reasons would you give to support the idea that Jesus Christ came to fight and came to win?

7. In what ways have you observed Satan taking hostages?

The Enemy Exposed

📖 Jesus had this sort of courage, because He knew about the Enemy and his motives. He said, "The thief comes only to steal and kill and destroy" (John 10:10). "He was a *murderer* from the beginning, not holding to the truth, for there is no truth in him. *When he lies, he speaks his native language,* for he is a liar and the father of lies" (John 8:44). 📖

1. From the passages in John, list the characteristics and actions of Satan.

2. Does Satan ever do anything good for anyone?

3. Because of what we know about Satan's personal qualities and actions, why is it so important for a soldier of Christ to distance himself from sin?

📖 Jesus studied Satan's true character and exposed it. He knew all of these games had one thing in common: Satan, the one who doesn't change his stripes. When you're tempted, do you think, *Satan*? Or do you think, *It's only fatigue; just a weak moment*? Maybe, but that's exactly where Jesus was in His moments of temptation too. And He didn't let Satan take advantage. 📖

4. What lies of Satan do you find difficult to resist?

5. What resources do you draw on to combat the lies of Satan that give you trouble?

The Devil's Checklists

Much like coaches for a football team might break down the film of the opposing team's players, I think Satan might have two lists of qualities that break down the soldiers from his enemy's squad. First I give you the list of weaknesses Satan looks for in a soldier of Christ:

- A man who swallows Satan's biggest lie: that he doesn't exist, is not active, and has been overblown by the spiritual nut jobs who see a demon under every rock.

- A man who filters everything he feels, sees, or experiences through natural, circumstantial, or material eyes instead of filtering it through eyes of faith and the great spiritual war for his life and the lives of others.

- A man who doesn't know his weapons of spiritual warfare, how to use them, when to use them, or that they even exist. Read Ephesians 6:10–18 in your Bible for weapons basics and applications.

- A man who allows Satan to freely oppress him and his faith through criticism, guilt, doubt, fear, or discouragement without a fight.

- A man who doesn't see Satan trying to hinder his growth and effectiveness by moving him away from spiritual disciplines.

- A man who doesn't realize that Satan and his forces tremble in the presence of God, the utterance of His word, and the sound of Jesus's name.

- A man who is unaware of his authority extended to him by Christ in order to exercise it for spiritual battle.

1. Which of these weaknesses do you find in your life?

2. Pause now and ask for God's help in strengthening areas of your life where you are vulnerable and weak.

Now let's get positive and look at the list of qualities Satan dreads in a soldier of Christ:

- A man who knows, above all, that spiritual warfare must be motivated by a deep love for God and people, as opposed to the struggle itself.
- A man who is personally aware of Satan's existence, tactics, power to influence, and goals in the lives of people.
- A man who is totally in love with truth and reality and therefore able to clearly spot twisted ideas, manipulations, half truths, irrational fears, and justifications for what they are—lies.
- A man who is constantly seeking a Christlike response in all his affairs. If Christ is already present in a certain area, Satan's angle is taken away in that area.
- A man who knows that Satan loves to make people too busy for quality relationships with God and people.
- A man who realizes his every choice that involves God and others is subject to spiritual warfare.
- A man who understands that the weakest link in this great battle for the kingdom of God is himself.
- A man who knows that Jesus Christ has bankrupted Satan's power through the blood spilled at the cross for sin.

- A man who knows that Satan loves to wear down an individual's resolve little by little over time.

3. Which of these are strengths in your life? Which of these qualities need more work in your life?

4. Offer a prayer of thanksgiving to God for the strengths and resources He has equipped you with to be a strong soldier in His battle.

Ready, Aim, Fire

To be an effective soldier in God's army, you need to understand the background and nature of the conflict, assess the nature and tactics of the enemy, and then train and equip yourself to fight to win. That's what we have done in this workbook session thus far.

Now it's time to don our gear, check our weapons, and follow our Captain into battle. Slam a round into the chamber—you are at the front.

Remember the God-Man who entered the jungle of temptation full of the Holy Spirit? That's the first key. He was whispered an offer as He looked into the face of the tempter in the wilderness. What'd He do? He unloaded both barrels by declaring, "It is written: 'Worship the Lord your God and serve him only'" (Luke 4:8).

Are you so filled with the Holy Spirit that you could also respond with force? Do you have Scripture loaded and ready in your heart? More important, do you use your weapon when tempted? The psalmist had this in mind when he wrote on the ancient scroll, "The mouth of the righteous man utters wisdom, and his tongue speaks what is just. The law of his God is in his heart; his feet do not slip" (Psalm 37:30–31).

This is your ammo as a spiritual warrior.

1. How would you describe the role of Scripture in spiritual warfare?

2. What could you do to make Scripture a more potent weapon in your spiritual battles?

Jesus showed His authority over the devil—and provided it to His followers: "When a strong man, fully armed, guards his own house, his possessions are safe. But *when someone stronger attacks and overpowers him,* he takes away the armor in which the man trusted and divides up the spoils" (Luke 11:21–22).

3. Reflect on the truth that you have the authority to overcome all the power of the Enemy. How might knowing your authority over Satan change your response to your daily spiritual battles?

Being God's man means being a man who is ready to engage in combat with the Enemy. More specifically, it means being prepared to fight the spiritual battles. The opposite of this is a casual Christian man who fails to "take your stand against the devil's schemes" (Ephesians 6:11), a man who capitulates on God's dream for you.

One measure of Christlikeness is your steady commitment to fight the unseen spiritual enemy. Do you proactively go after the evil and sin in your own life and others' wherever it raises its head? Maybe you wonder how a man can be this confident. It's found in the warrior spirit and character of Jesus, a.k.a. Lion of the Tribe of Judah, who lives—and lives in you! This is the Man who chose death and stood firm against the devil's assaults. And He has called you out to do the same.

This is profound. God's dream for you is to possess this same soldier heart by training in His shoes. Watch His film. Study His responses. Scrutinize the Enemy's tactics. Imitate Him and integrate His skills.

4. How does Satan attack your mind?

5. At what times or in what situations are your defenses against Satan more likely down?

📖 Satan hates a guy who's on guard and sees everyday choices as tactical maneuvers. Forgiving someone versus attacking, saying no to unhealthy appetites versus feeding them, encouraging versus tearing down. Choosing not to work late versus straining family relationships. Choosing Christlike approaches to problems versus justifying different courses. The daily stuff is where the dream is worked out—day to day, moment by moment. 📖

6. In what areas of your life do you want to become a more effective soldier for Christ?

We are in the middle of a vicious war. Satan and his fellow terrorists attack us from all sides. Some days all we can see is the blood flowing from a multitude of wounds. The casualties mount. But as we tighten the tourniquets and reload our weapons, we must never forget how this war will end.

📖 A terrifying day is coming when our jaws will drop in awe. All will behold the Rider. And He's not bringing flowers to the party.

"I saw heaven standing open and there before me was a white horse, whose rider is called Faithful and True. With justice he judges and makes war. His eyes are like blazing fire, and on his head are many crowns. He has a name written on him that no one knows but he himself. He is dressed in a robe dipped in blood, and his name is the Word of God. The armies of heaven were following him, riding on white horses and dressed in fine linen, white and clean. Out of his mouth comes a sharp sword with which to strike down the nations. "He will rule them with an iron scepter." He treads the winepress of the fury of the wrath of God Almighty. On his robe and on his thigh he has this name written: KING OF KINGS AND LORD OF LORDS" (Revelation 19:11–16). 📖

Dream Discipline

Remember

Therefore put on the full armor of God, so that when the day of evil comes, you may be able to stand your ground, and after you have done everything, to stand. (Ephesians 6:13)

Reflect

1. As you encounter various challenges in life, who and what are your real enemies?

2. What does it mean to put on the armor of God? (See Ephesians 6:10–18.)

Respond

Whether you like it or not, you are a combatant in a vicious war. During this week, ask the Holy Spirit to show you where the battlefronts are in your life. Make a list to share with your accountability partner.

Dream Debriefing (Man to Man)

Catch up on events in both of your lives. What answers to prayer have you each experienced of late?

1. What situations did you encounter this week that prove to you that you are at war (see Respond)?
2. Share ideas on how each of you can combat Satan and his forces.
3. Ask each other, "What does it mean for you to put on the whole armor of God?"
4. Pray for each other. Ask God to help your brother stand strong against the schemes of the devil.

Dream Interpretation (Small Group Discussion)

1. There are a number of ways that we refer to Jesus—Shepherd, Savior, Lamb of God, King, and so on. We less often call Him a fighter or a warrior. Why do you think we do not talk as much about Jesus as a war combatant?
2. Poll the guys in the group: In your daily lives, how real does spiritual warfare seem? Explain your answers.
3. What are some major spiritual battles that Christian men face today?
4. Paul used a soldier metaphor to describe how a Christian can equip himself for spiritual war. Read these verses from Ephesians 6:

Finally, be strong in the Lord and in his mighty power. Put on the full armor of God so that you can take your stand against the devil's schemes. For our struggle is not against flesh and blood, but against the rulers, against the authorities, against the powers of this dark world and against the spiritual forces of evil in the heavenly realms. Therefore put on the full armor of God, so that when the day of evil comes, you may be able to stand your ground, and after you have done everything, to stand. Stand firm then, with the belt of truth buckled around your waist, with the breastplate of righteousness in place, and with your feet fitted with the readiness that comes from the gospel of peace. In addition to all this, take up the shield of faith, with which you can extinguish all the flaming arrows of the evil one. Take the helmet of salvation and the sword of the Spirit, which is the word of God. And pray in the Spirit on all occasions with all kinds of prayers and requests. With this in mind, be alert and always keep on praying for all the saints. (verses 10–18)

Discuss together how the following actions are accomplished by warriors for Christ today:

- belt of truth buckled around your waist
- breastplate of righteousness strapped in place
- feet fitted with the gospel of peace
- shield of faith gripped
- helmet of salvation put on
- sword of the Spirit wielded

5. How can men help their brothers fight spiritual battles?

 **Dream and Do**

Here's what needs to happen before the next small group meeting:

1. Complete your personal study of session 8, which includes reading chapters 14 and 15 in *Dream*.
2. Meet with your accountability partner.

3. Accomplish the task you listed under Respond in the Dream Discipline section on page 144.

4. Record any of your observations in the Dream Journal.

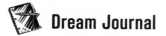 **Dream Journal**

_____

_____

_____

_____

_____

_____

_____

_____

_____

_____

well...done!

This week's session is based on chapter 14, "No Thanks," and chapter 15, "The Time Has Come," in Dream.

I don't know about you, but I'm tired of hearing about contemporary Christians, famous and not so famous, who do not finish the earthly part of their journey with God very well. How I long to stand before the King, still wearing my combat boots and fatigues, stained with blood and gunpowder from my last skirmish with the dark forces on earth, and hear Him say, "Well done, my good and faithful servant!"

I'm just smart enough to realize, though, that an attitude of humility and watchfulness is required for me to reach the finish line with heart clean and head high. What is the path to hearing, "Well done"? In this final session, let's unpack that together.

 **Dream Analysis**

"Begin with the end in mind," Stephen Covey wrote in his best-selling book *The Seven Habits of Highly Effective People*. That's also good advice for Christians who want to be highly effective in finishing their time on earth well. Jesus said something like that: "For where your treasure is, there your heart will be also" (Luke 12:34).

Christ's clear statement was that earth is a layover. That perspective produces a very practical spiritual paradigm of spiritual aggression that views choices on earth as an investment in our homes and hopes.

The Sermon on the Mount is Article I: "Don't hoard treasure down here where it gets eaten by moths and corroded by rust or—worse!—stolen by burglars. Stockpile treasure in heaven, where it's safe from moth and rust and burglars. It's obvious, isn't it? The place where your treasure is, is the place you will most want to be, and end up being" (Matthew 6:19–21, MSG).

1. How important is life after death to the average person? What reasons would you list for your answer?

2. How often do you think about heaven and storing treasures there?

It's about remembering who you are—and whose you are. It's the knowledge of where you come from and where you are going that's essential for practical, day-to-day Christian faith. When you have clearly settled the answers to these questions, you can be spiritually aggressive without apology—even ruthless with respect to personal commitments and boundaries.

God's man can risk mightily for his hopes and dreams—but always in the direction of home....

The big question for you today is this: what are your greatest hopes in this life? The risks you take tell all. If you love people, you will take risks to make those relationships healthy and intimate. By contrast, if you love heroin, you manipulate, steal, and take inconceivable risks to get more money to get back to your home—the next fix. But if you love God, you take risks with your choices that show where you are from and where you are headed.

God's man, like the God-Man, risks forceful choices in the direction of his ultimate hope of heaven.

3. What risks might a God's man take because he knows where he came from and where he is going?

4. What significant risks have you taken, both for the kingdom and in other ways?

Our bond with [Jesus's] mission was sealed in His own prayer for us that our full mission would come about and God's dream would be realized: "I have given them your word and the world has hated them, for they are not of the world any more than I am of the world. My prayer is not that you take them out of the world but that you protect them from the evil one. They are not of the world, even as I am not of it.... As you sent me into the world, I have sent them into the world" (John 17:14–16, 18)....

The picture we get of Jesus is movement toward His ultimate destiny. Every man wants to finish strong, but few do—Christian leaders included. Yet God's dream is for our lives to be driven by an exceptional destiny, mirroring that of Christ's as a born finisher.

5. What will finishing your life strong for God look like? Make a list of the character qualities and actions you want evident as you head for home.

6. What does it mean to you that in His prayer for his followers, Jesus asked that we not be taken out of the world but be protected from the evil one?

How Did Jesus Do It?

📖 Jesus came from God as a citizen of heaven. He longed for the time He would return home. His cure for worldliness was always bringing to mind His true home, the eternal place He knew was far more glorious than whatever He was giving up for it. He impressed upon others His personal knowledge of heaven and His awareness of its promise for all who would believe. And by His choices to risk earth for heaven, we got a clear picture of who He was and where He was headed, making what He might have possessed instead or what was said about Him by people pale in insignificance. Everyone who Christ encountered saw it: that firm gaze on an eternal kingdom that made it easy to say "no thanks" to every temptation away from His true home. Jesus was not worldly, because this world was not His home, not His hope. 📖

1. List some words of Jesus or incidents from His life that prove He was truly a citizen of heaven.

Since Jesus is our supreme example of what is required to finish life well, I have compiled a list of things Jesus did to keep His life on the right track. I know this list is not exhaustive, but I think you'll find these five reasons why Jesus finished well to be instructive for your own journey.

📖 *Jesus walked meaningfully with God to the end.* "Father, the time has come. Glorify your Son, that your Son may glorify you" (John 17:1). Everything He'd previously done coalesced in this final act. He did it all for His Father: every sacrifice, every prayer, every healing, every message, every interaction. His life made perfect sense in the context of this—it was the wrap-up of a life lived well for God. 📖

2. How have you seen God glorified in various circumstances in your life thus far?

📖 *Jesus used His specific influence for God's purposes.* "For you granted [Jesus] authority over all people that he might give eternal life to all those you have given him. Now this is eternal life: that they may know you, the only true God, and Jesus Christ, whom you have sent" (John 17:2–3). Jesus was given authority to influence people for eternity in a specific historical, geographical, and ethnic context. To faithfully steward that God-given authority, He used His influence to consistently honor God with His life of service. Your life, too, is not one of compartmentalized contributions. It is a complete lifestyle. Finishing well requires a unified focus—a steady and disciplined consistency of commitment to allow God to use you wherever you are. 📖

3. In what ways do you exert influence over other people?

4. How would you describe the kingdom results of the influence you have on others?

Jesus was "on mission." "I have brought you glory on earth by completing the work you gave me to do" (John 17:4). When you're "on mission," you are not at home. Earth is an extended camping trip—a place you're visiting for a while to engage and then to leave. No one buys a bunch of stuff and settles in on a camping trip. No, you make do and focus on what you are there for—exploring, discovering, creating, adventure. Jesus was similarly focused, doing those things He could before He left. On earth He could bring God glory through His actions. In heaven, His chance to work for the Father on earth would be over. Jesus was not concerned with comfort, power, wealth, or enjoyment.

You finish well by striving to bring Him glory in all you are, have, and do and by completing His assignment with your particular skills, passions, personality, and experiences.

5. What do you believe are the kingdom activities God has given you to do on your camping trip?

📖 *Jesus looked forward to His Father's smile.* "And now, Father, glorify me in your presence with the glory I had with you before the world began" (John 17:5). Completing a job well distinguishes a man and leaves a lasting impression. Jesus impressed His Dad. He defeated sin and secured salvation for all men. His relationship with the Father would take on that old familiar rhythm, free of earth's gravity. Jesus had nothing to prove to anybody, allowing Him to finish strong. 📖

📖 *Jesus trained others to carry God's purposes forward.* "I have revealed you to those whom you gave me out of the world. They were yours; you gave them to me and they have obeyed your word. Now they know that everything you have given me comes from you. For I gave them the words you gave me and they accepted them. They knew with certainty that I came from you, and they believed that you sent me.… My prayer is not for them alone. I pray also for those who will believe in me through their message" (John 17:6–8, 20). A Father deploys His Son. His Son comes to earth and trains more sons. And to this day, the spiritual chain reaction has not died. Our purpose is to reach and train other men to live for God and fulfill His purposes. 📖

6. What experiences have you had in discipling others on how to live the Christian life?

7. In the coming days, pray that God will show you others you can touch for Him. List the names of people God has put in your life or on your heart to disciple.

Finish Strong

Let's get to the nitty-gritty. We have looked at how Jesus pulled off His magnificent life. But how about you and me? What's this finishing-strong thing going to look like in real twenty-first century? I have some thoughts.

God's dream for our lives is Christlikeness. Christlikeness involves hard choices in the direction of our hopes of our eternal home.…

Finishing well and fulfilling God's ultimate dream for your life means disciplining yourself like Jesus did during your camping trip on earth. Jim Rohn comments on the value of discipline and finishing well when he says, "Discipline weighs ounces while regret weighs tons." Think about it. Discipline in your commitment to being God's man and living out God's dream of Christlikeness will far outweigh the regret of getting to the end and wishing you had.

1. Sometimes a word like *Christlike* loses its meaning from overuse. What does seeking Christlikeness mean to you?

📖 If staying disciplined is critical to fulfilling God's ultimate dream for us, we should look at the barriers and study how great leaders have overcome them to finish well. A finisher is rare. Even in the Bible, you can write off roughly two-thirds of all leaders from how they ended up. Only one-third were able to avoid the pitfalls that have derailed men for centuries. In my interactions with leaders, there are common denominators that cause them to fall before reaching the finish line:

- moral failure caused by a lack of authenticity and accountability
- financial concerns that prevented acceptance of their mission
- positional or power struggles over a title within a hierarchy
- spiritual atrophy when basic devotional disciplines diminish
- intellectual stagnation—they simply stopped learning

These patches of quicksand are avoidable if love for Christ and pursuit of God's dream remain the most important focus. Each is rooted in pride, making men unwilling to submit fully to God's plan, whether it's in worship, fellowship accountability, spiritual discipline, or learning to change. 📖

2. Review the list of common denominators leading to a late-journey stumble. Which of these might be more of a temptation to you?

📖 Those who finish well have:

- *a personal mission.* He learns about God's priorities in the world and eagerly aligns his skills and talents with them to the end.

- *consistent spiritual discipline.* He has a steady (not flashy) commitment to prayer, study, worship, community, accountability, service, and sharing the good news.
- *a teachable spirit.* He takes notes, listens, and integrates new truth daily from multiple sources.
- *an urgency trained on eternity.* He manages his time well, taught by God to number his days.
- *an active search for more of heaven, less of earth.* He's past proving anything to anyone. He has an audience of One. He has stopped caring what people think.

3. Again, look at the second list: Make note of the factors that you believe are strong for you. Also pay attention to factors that you need to strengthen in your walk with God.

Die Climbing

There's an epitaph for a Swiss mountain guide that stands at the bottom of the mountain that claimed his life. It reads, "He died climbing."

This should be our goal as God's men each day as we move away from our base camp on earth toward home—that we died climbing toward God's call to become like Christ. Paul had this mind-set when he penned this ascent from a prison cell: "Not that I have already obtained all this, or have already been made perfect, but I press on to take hold of that for which Christ Jesus took hold of me. Brothers, I do not consider myself yet to have taken hold of it. But one thing I do: Forgetting what is behind and straining toward what is ahead, I press on toward the goal to win the prize for which God has *called me heavenward in Christ Jesus*" (Philippians 3:12–14).

1. What do you think it will look like for you to continue becoming more like Christ?

2. When you end your camping trip on earth, what would you like your epitaph to say?

God's dream is to see you reach that summit.

And they admitted that they were aliens and strangers on earth. People who say such things show that they are looking for a country of their own. If they had been thinking of the country they had left, they would have had opportunity to return. Instead, they were longing for a better country—a heavenly one. Therefore, God is not ashamed to be called their God, for he has prepared a city for them. (Hebrews 11:13–16)

 Dream Discipline

Remember

For where your treasure is, there your heart will be also. (Luke 12:34)

Reflect

1. What do you consider to be your treasure?

2. Where is your heart now, heaven or earth?

Respond

This session marks the end of our study of what God's dreams are for us. Page through this workbook. List here a half dozen or so of the more important things you have learned, the big ideas or behavior changers that you do not want to forget.

Dream Debriefing (Man to Man)

Catch up on what's been going on.

1. Share with each other how the spiritual warfare has gone since your last meeting. Have you noticed more of it? Has it been more intense? How have you counter-attacked?
2. This session is about finishing the Christian life well. Ask each other what you think might be the major challenges to staying the course.

3. Are you going to keep meeting one on one now that this workbook is complete? That would be a good idea. Talk it over. There are many other great books and study guides you could use to spur your discussions. I urge you to make the commitment to remain in an accountability relationship. Close in prayer.

Dream Interpretation (Small Group Discussion)

1. Thomas Watson said, "The world is but a great inn, where we are to stay a night or two, and be gone; what madness is it to get our heart upon our inn, as to forget our home!" Why is our life on earth a stay of only a night or two?
2. The author of Hebrews wrote about believers, "And they admitted that they were aliens and strangers on earth" (Hebrews 11:13). As a group, offer ideas on what it means to be an alien or stranger on earth.
3. If we are to finish our lives well, what habits and disciplines should we make a part of our Christian walk now?
4. What are some attitudes, habits, and behaviors that work against finishing life well?
5. Share some stories of men you knew or heard about who stayed faithful to Christ and finished life well.
6. Ask each man to share the one thing he believes God wants him to accomplish before the promotion to heaven.

Dream and Do

The workbook is complete, so there's no assignment.

I encourage you to keep seeking God's dreams for you. What could be better than to finish your time here on earth, and as you stand before the King, to hear Him say, "Well done! You understood My dreams and saw it fulfilled."

> For we are God's workmanship, created in Christ Jesus to do good works, which God prepared in advance for us to do (Ephesians 2:10).

Amen to that.

Be strong my brother. Finish well.

 **Dream Journal**

Men become men in the company of men.

God is calling all of us to eternal and essential connections. He is calling us to scale new heights and go to the next level. Strong connections with God and other men produces the character of Jesus Christ. Weak connections produce lukewarm results and many times lead to destructive cycles in our lives. But, how do you get connected? How do you stay connected in an everyday world so it's not just a "mountain top" experience—but a radical change in the way you do life?

Discover the power to change into the man you want to be—and the man God intended you to be—at the Everyman Conference.

everyman
conference

your plan for character, connection and completion in Christ

with Speaker and Author
Kenny Luck

The God's Man series

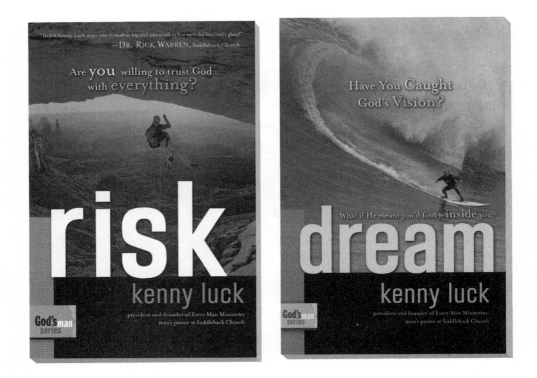

The first two books in the new God's Man series for men who are ready to go to the next level in their faith. Companion workbooks also available.

What if your dreams are God's way of bringing *life and hope* to others?

At Open Doors we hear the cries of Christians around the world who share our faith, but not our freedom. Governmental persecution and public humiliation make it hard for them to dream. And yet, their faith in Christ continues to uphold them, even as their courage calls us to re-examine the stuff of our dreams.

So, dream big, but dare to dream beyond yourself, beyond your world.

Investment of your time, money, and prayer will enable the persecuted Church to share the dream.

Open*Doors*®
Serving persecuted **Christians** worldwide

1-888-524-2535 • OpenDoorsUSA.org

To learn more about WaterBrook Press and view
our catalog of products, log on to our Web site:
www.waterbrookpress.com

WATERBROOK
PRESS